ID405738

Also by Joel Osteen

# BREAK
## OUT!

DAILY READINGS FROM

# BREAK OUT!

*365 Devotions to Go Beyond Your
Barriers and Live an Extraordinary Life.*

## JOEL OSTEEN

FaithWords

Unless otherwise indicated, all Scripture quotations are taken from *The Holy Bible, New International Version*® NIV®. Copyright © 1973, 1978, 1984, 2011 by Biblica, Inc.™ Used by permission. All rights reserved worldwide.

Scripture quotations noted NLT are taken from the *Holy Bible*, New Living Translation, copyright © 1996, 2004, 2007 by Tyndale House Foundation. Used by permission of Tyndale House Publishers, Inc., Carol Stream, Illinois 60188. All rights reserved.

Scripture quotations noted NKJV are taken from the *New King James Version* of the Bible. Copyright © 1982 by Thomas Nelson, Inc. Used by permission. All rights reserved.

Scripture quotations noted AMP are from *The Amplified Bible*. Copyright © 1954, 1958, 1962, 1964, 1965, 1987 by The Lockman Foundation. All rights reserved. Used by permission. (www.Lockman.org)

Scripture quotations noted KJV are from the King James Version of the Holy Bible.

Literary development and design: Koechel Peterson & Associates, Inc., Minneapolis, Minnesota.

This book have been adapted from *Break Out!*, copyright © 2013 by Joel Osteen. Published by FaithWords.

FaithWords
Hachette Book Group USA
237 Park Avenue, New York, NY 10017
www.faithwords.com.

Printed in the United States of America

First Print: October 2014

10 9 8 7 6 5 4 3 2 1

FaithWords is a division of Hachette Book Group, Inc. The FaithWords name and logo are trademarks of Hachette Book Group, Inc.

The Hachette Speakers Bureau provides a wide range of authors for speaking events. To find out more, go to www.hachettespeakersbureau.com or call (866) 376-6591.

The publisher is not responsible for websites (or their content) that are not owned by the publisher.

Library of Congress Control Number: 2014935350

ISBN: 978-0-89296-975-3

## Now to Him

*who is able to do*
*exceedingly abundantly above all*
*that we ask or think,*
*according to the power*
*that works in us . . .*

EPHESIANS 3:20 NKJV

# INTRODUCTION

We were not created to just get by with average, unrewarding, or unfulfilling lives. God created us to leave our marks on our generations. Every person has seeds of greatness planted within by the Creator.

So when life weighs upon us, pushing us down, limiting our thinking, labeling us in negative ways, how do we break out and go beyond our barriers of the ordinary into the extraordinary lives we were designed to live? How do we overcome the weariness, discouragements, and setbacks and rise above into the fullness of our destinies?

The key to breaking out is to believe that we have what it takes. When we break through in our minds, believing we can rise higher and overcome obstacles, then God will unleash the power within that will break the power of all that is stealing our joy and keeping us from God's abundant life.

Sometimes you need words of faith and victory spoken over your life. Words have created power. When you receive them into your spirit, they can ignite seeds of increase on the inside. That's the reason I've written this devotional—to provide you with practical steps and encouragement for creating a life without limitations.

My friend, over the next 365 days, I'd like for you to take the journey of a lifetime together with me and explore five powerful keys for your life: to believe bigger, to consider God rather than circumstances, to pray God-sized prayers, to keep the right perspective, and to not settle for good enough. You will find a wealth of Scriptures, inspirational quotations, selected stories, and points for contemplation. All are provided to engage you in a process of reflection that will enhance your faith and lead you to positive actions.

These devotions are written to inspire you in your daily walk with God. While they are not meant to replace your personal time with God, it is my desire that the readings will be keys you can use to unlock doors leading to a fuller life. I hope they will be a springboard to help you draw nearer to God and to help you overcome the challenges or barriers that might keep you from breaking out into your best life.

Your life can be transformed and renewed as you allow God's Word to refresh and to reshape your thinking, speaking, and daily activities. Allow the Scriptures to speak to your heart. Be still and listen to what God is saying to you. Day by day, the barriers that hold you back will begin to loosen and fall off your life. No matter where you are or what challenges you face, you can start to break free right now!

DAILY READINGS FROM

# BREAK
# OUT!

## The Year of the Lord's Favor

*He has sent me to bind up the brokenhearted, to proclaim freedom for the captives and release from darkness for the prisoners, to proclaim the year of the LORD's favor . . .*

ISAIAH 61:1-2

Isaiah said it was the year of the Lord's favor. Not next year. Not five years. Not in the Sweet By and By. This is the year God will shift things in your favor. He is lining it all up. What you could not make happen on your own, God will cause you to accomplish. It will be bigger than you thought. It will happen quicker than you imagined, and it will be more rewarding than you ever dreamed possible.

One touch of God's favor can get you to where you're supposed to be. The truth is, you are one shift from seeing a dream come to pass. One shift from paying your house off. One shift from seeing your health improve. One shift from meeting the right person.

## Get Ready

*"I am about to do something new. See, I have already begun!*
*Do you not see it? I will make a pathway through the wilderness.*
*I will create rivers in the dry wasteland."*

ISAIAH 43:19 NLT

You may feel like you're stuck right now. You could never accomplish a dream, never overcome a problem. It's just been too long. You've missed too many opportunities. But God is saying, "Get ready. I'm about to shift things." Doors will open for you that have not opened in the past. Those who were against you will suddenly change their minds and be for you. Problems that have dogged you for years will suddenly turn around. You are coming into a shift. Because you have honored God, He will put you in a position you never could have attained on your own. It's not just your education, not just your talent, or the family you come from. It's the hand of God shifting you to a new level of your destiny.

# JANUARY 3

## Break Out

*Now faith is confidence in what we hope for and assurance about what we do not see.*

HEBREWS 11:1

Sometimes you need faith and victory spoken over your life. Words have created power. When you receive them into your spirit, they can ignite seeds of increase on the inside. That's the reason I've written these daily readings. You were not created to just get by with an average, unrewarding, or unfulfilling life. God created you to leave your mark on this generation. You have gifts and talents that you have not tapped into. There are new levels of your destiny still in front of you. But *break out starts in your thinking.* As you put these keys into action, making room for increase, expecting shifts of God's favor, praying bold prayers, and keeping the right perspective, then God will release floods of His goodness that will thrust you beyond barriers of the past into the extraordinary life you were designed to live.

**Seeing God**

*By faith he left Egypt, not fearing the king's anger; he persevered because he saw him who is invisible.*

HEBREWS 11:27

I'm declaring, "A shift is coming." A shift in your health, finances, or a relationship. It may not look like it in the natural, but we serve a supernatural God. He's about to breathe in your direction in a new way. God's favor is being released in a new way. It will propel you forward. What should have taken you forty years to accomplish, God will do in a split second.

The shift will take you where you could not have gone on your own. The shift is overcoming what a medical report said was impossible. The shift is having your best year when the circumstances say you should have a down year. The shift is seeing God not only provide but also do exceedingly, abundantly, above and beyond.

*Why, my soul, are you
downcast? Why so disturbed
within me? Put your hope in
God, for I will yet praise him,
my Savior and my God.*

PSALM 42:11

## This Is a New Day

You need to check doors that have been closed to you in the past. Things have shifted. The dream you had to start a new business, to go back to college, to take a mission trip—it may not have happened the first time, but that's okay. It's prepared you for this time. Don't give up. This is a new day. Things have shifted. Pursue your dream again.

When God breathes in your direction, people change their mind. Closed doors suddenly open. The *no*s turn into *yes*es. *Not now* turns into *It's your time.*

Your new attitude should be: "God, I'm ready. I'm taking the limits off of You. I'm enlarging my vision. I may not see a way, but I know You have a way. I declare I'm coming into a shift."

## Sudden Change

*I entreated Your favor with my whole heart; be merciful to me according to Your word.*

PSALM 119:58 NKJV

A construction manager I know had been out of a job for three years after twenty-five years of steady work at a successful company. He finally took a much lower-level position with another company that started to take a toll on his health, marriage, and savings. It looked like his job situation would never change. But about six months later, his former boss called. His old company had landed the largest contract in its history. He not only got his job back but also all of his benefits plus a significant salary increase and now he works locally. He said, "This is exceedingly, abundantly, above and beyond!"

He came into a shift. Suddenly, things changed in his favor. One contract. He went from barely getting by to having more than enough.

## To Find Favor

*The LORD had made the Egyptians favorably disposed toward the people, and they gave them what they asked for; so they plundered the Egyptians.*

EXODUS 12:36

The Israelites were enslaved for many years and mistreated by their captors. They were forced to work long hours and beaten with rods when they didn't meet their quotas. But one day, through a series of events, God supernaturally brought them out. Notice, God caused them to have favor with the same people who had oppressed and mistreated them for years. They said in effect, "We've decided that we want to be good to you now." Before they left, the captors gave the Israelites their gold, silver, and jewels.

What happened? The Israelites came into a shift. God changed the mind of their enemy. Proverbs says God can turn the heart of a king. We may not be able to change people's minds, but God can. He controls the whole universe.

## Help Rather Than Hinder

*In the Lord's hand the king's heart is a stream of water that he channels toward all who please him.*

PROVERBS 21:1

You may have people in your life who don't like you, a boss who is hard to get along with or a family member who is disrespectful. It's easy to become discouraged and to think, "This will always be this way. They will always be against me."

No, stay in faith. God has a shift coming. He knows how to cause them to see you in a new light. When God shifts things, they'll go out of their way to be good to you. Instead of hindering you, they'll help you. Bottom line: God will not allow any person to keep you from your destiny. They may be bigger, stronger, or more powerful, but God knows how to shift things around and get you to where you're supposed to be.

*For by You I can run against a troop, by my God I can leap over a wall.*

PSALM 18:29 NKJV

## Over, Around, or Through

I have a friend who worked for a young supervisor who was condescending and a source of frustration. It looked like the supervisor would be there for another twenty years. My friend has a good attitude, but deep down wasn't sure he could take it. Then, one morning the management announced that the supervisor's wife had been transferred to another state for her job, and he had resigned. What happened? A divine shift. Suddenly, God changed things.

Quit worrying about those trying to hold you back. God knows how to move the wrong people out of your life and bring the right people in. And even if God doesn't move them, God can cause you to go over them, or around them, or even through them, to get you where you're supposed to be.

## To the Front

*But Israel reached out his right hand and put it on Ephraim's head, though he was the younger, and crossing his arms, he put his left hand on Manasseh's head, even though Manasseh was the firstborn.*

GENESIS 48:14

JANUARY

# 10

When Jacob blessed the sons of Joseph, he purposefully crossed his hands and gave Ephraim the firstborn blessing. He was saying, "Ephraim may have been in the back and is not next in line, but I'm shifting him to a new position. I'm taking him from the back up to the front. I will give him what he doesn't deserve."

That's the way our God is. He has shifts in your future that will put you in positions you didn't earn, you didn't qualify for, or weren't next in line to receive. But God will cross His hands and say, "I will move you up from the back to the front, from not being qualified to suddenly being qualified, from being looked down on or disrespected to being honored and seen with influence and credibility."

## All That You Need

# 11

*The LORD . . . said, "Go in the strength you have and save Israel . . ." Gideon replied, "But how can I save Israel? My clan is the weakest . . ." The LORD answered, "I will be with you."*

JUDGES 6:14–16

We can all make excuses that we don't have the talent, the personality, or the confidence to move ahead. But God says, "I know all that. I created you, but I'm about to bless you in such a way that everyone will know it's Me and not you." Now don't talk yourself out of it.

Moses said, "God, I stutter. I can't speak to Pharaoh." Gideon said, "I come from the poorest family. I can't lead this army." David could have said, "I'm too small, too young, too inexperienced to face Goliath." Esther could have said, "I can't go in and speak to the king. I don't have any influence." And God would have said what He's saying to you, "I will give you all that you need—the respect, credibility, and honor that you didn't deserve or work for."

## If You Only Knew

*"What no eye has seen, what no ear has heard,*
*and what no human mind has conceived"—*
*the things God has prepared for those who love him . . .*

1 CORINTHIANS 2:9

God has shifts in your future that if He showed you now you wouldn't believe. It's exceedingly, abundantly, above and beyond. You think you're hitting on all cylinders, but if you only knew what God has in store. It's like you're in second gear, but God is about to shift you into overdrive. You will see the surpassing greatness of God's favor.

Because you've honored God and lived with excellence and integrity, God will take you beyond your training, beyond your education, beyond your income, beyond where anyone in your family has gone before you. This shift will put you at a place where you look back and say, "Wow, God! You have amazed me with Your goodness." Start expecting unprecedented favor, believing for God to do something new in your life.

## No Limits

*Now a wind went out from the LORD and
drove quail in from the sea. It scattered them up
to two cubits deep all around the camp . . .*

NUMBERS 11:31

When the Israelites were in the desert headed toward the Promised Land, they had manna to eat each day. It was similar to bread. After a while they complained that they didn't have any meat to eat. God said, "Moses, I will give you meat for a whole month." Moses said, "God, that's impossible. There are two million people out here." God replied, "Moses, is there any limit to My power?" He was saying, "Just because you don't see a way doesn't mean I don't have a way."

That's what God did. He shifted the wind and brought quail to them. God knows how to shift things so that blessings come to you. The right people search you out. Good breaks find you.

## The Breath of God

> *"'Not by might nor by power, but by my Spirit,' says the Lord Almighty."*
>
> ZECHARIAH 4:6

Zechariah's word *spirit* in the Hebrew means "breath." It's saying it will not happen just by your talent, just by your connections, just by those you know. It will happen because God breathes in our direction. God shifts the winds and blows healing, promotion, and restoration our way.

How will you get well? The medical report says it's impossible? No, God is breathing healing your way. Health, wholeness, and restoration are headed toward you. How will you accomplish your dreams? You may not know the right people or have the money or feel like you have the talent. But God is breathing ideas, resources, and the right people.

If you will stay faithful and just keep honoring God, suddenly things will change, suddenly you come into abundance, suddenly you get well.

> *But I trust in you, LORD; I say, "You are my God." My times are in your hands; deliver me from the hands of my enemies, from those who pursue me.*
>
> PSALM 31:14–15

## In God's Time

A few years ago, one of our faithful church members suffered a major stroke that paralyzed the left-hand side of his body. He couldn't walk or talk and was told that with intense therapy he might regain his speech, but he would never walk again. For two years he had no feeling on the left side of his body, but he kept coming to Lakewood. He knew all God had to do was shift the winds and blow healing his way.

One morning he suddenly began to have feeling on the left side of his body. The medical personnel were amazed. A few weeks later, he walked into Lakewood as though nothing had ever been wrong. What happened? God breathed in his direction. What he could not do in his own power suddenly became possible.

## Suddenly

*He did this that He might clearly demonstrate through the ages to come the immeasurable (limitless, surpassing) riches of His free grace (His unmerited favor) in [His] kindness and goodness of heart toward us in Christ Jesus.*

EPHESIANS 2:7 AMP

## JANUARY 16

You may have struggled in an area—your health, your finances, with a relationship—for a long time, and you keep wondering, "Will this ever change?" God is saying, "Yes. A shift is coming. I'm about to give you what you do not deserve."

Because you have been faithful and honored God, I believe and declare, God will put you in a position you could have never gotten to on your own. Doors will open that have never opened before for you. What should have taken you forty years to accomplish, God will do in a split second. You're coming into acceleration.

Suddenly, a dream comes to pass. Suddenly, a promise is fulfilled. Suddenly, the negative turns around. You need to get ready for the surpassing greatness of God's favor!

## Overflow

*I came that they may have and enjoy life, and have it in abundance (to the full, till it overflows).*

JOHN 10:10 AMP

You may have experienced bad breaks, disappointments, and heartache in the past. It's easy to become discouraged and let negative thoughts overwhelm you. But I'm here to announce to you that you're under a Flash Flood Warning. Conditions are just right. You've honored God. You've been faithful. Now God is saying, "You will see a flood of My goodness beyond your expectations. It puts you into overflow."

You will see the surpassing greatness of God's favor. It will take you beyond your normal boundaries. It will supersede what the medical report says. It will supersede your talent, your education, and your experience. It won't be a little drizzle or a little sprinkle. It will be a flood of favor, a flood of talent, a flood of ideas, a flood of opportunities.

## The God of the Break-through

*"God has broken through my enemies by my hand like a breakthrough of water."*

1 CHRONICLES 14:11 NKJV

King David faced an impossible situation. He and his men were up against this huge army—the Philistines. They were greatly outnumbered and had little or no chance of winning. David asked God for help, and God gave David the promise that He would go with them and they would defeat the opposing army, which is exactly what happened. God gave them such a breakthrough victory that David compared it to "the bursting forth of water."

David named the place of his great victory Baal-Perazim, which means "the God of the breakthrough." He was saying when the God of the breakthrough shows up and releases His power, it will be like a flood of His goodness, a flood of His favor, a flood of healing, a flood of new opportunity.

> *Then Caleb quieted the people before Moses, and said, "Let us go up at once and take possession, for we are well able to overcome it."*

## Nothing Will Stop You

NUMBERS 13:30 NKJV

You may have obstacles that look impassable or dreams that look unattainable. But know this: When God releases a flood of His power, nothing will be able to stop you. You may not have the connections or have the funding to accomplish your dreams. But when God releases a flood of favor, you won't have to look for people to help you out. Good breaks, opportunity, and the right people will all search you out.

You need to get ready, not for a trickle, not a stream, not a river, but a flood of God's favor, a tidal wave of God's goodness, a tsunami of His increase. God is going to take you to a level that you've never been before. It will be unprecedented. You will go farther and quicker than you've ever dreamed.

## Awesome

*Then the LORD said: "I am making a covenant with you.*
*Before all your people I will do wonders never before done in*
*any nation in all the world. The people you live among will see*
*how awesome is the work that I, the LORD, will do for you."*

EXODUS 34:10

When God uses the word *awesome*, He is talking about a flood of favor, ideas, and healing. It may not feel like it, but remember you're under a Flash Flood Warning. Any moment the heavens could open up. Any moment you could meet the right person. Any moment God could do something awesome, something that you've never seen before in your life.

The real question is: Will you let this seed take root? God has you here at the right place, at the right time, because He wants to do something amazing in your life. Get in agreement and say, "God, this is for me today. I'm raising my expectations. I'm shaking off doubt, negativity, disappointments, self-pity, little dreams, and little goals, and I will make room for a flood of Your goodness."

## The Final Say

*"See, I have engraved you on the palms of my hands . . ."*

ISAIAH 49:16

I met a lady who was scheduled to have a tumor removed at MD Anderson, our local cancer hospital. Although the tumor was very clear on her hometown hospital's x-rays, the surgeon had her retake all the tests and x-rays to verify everything. After reviewing the new tests, he couldn't find the tumor at all. "I've been doing this for twenty-six years," he said. "I've never seen anything like this before."

What was that? A flood of healing and restoration. God can do what medicine cannot do. He made your body. He has you in the palm of His hand. Sickness doesn't determine how long you will live; God has the final say. Nothing can snatch you out of His hand. You may be facing a major illness, but at any moment God could turn that around.

## The Spirit of God

*When the enemy comes in like a flood, the Spirit of the LORD will lift up a standard against him.*

ISAIAH 59:19 NKJV

Several commentators believe that the comma in our verse from Isaiah was misplaced during translation. They believe it should say, "When the enemy comes in, like a flood the Spirit of the LORD will lift up a standard against him." In other words, the flood imagery emphasizes God's power and not the enemy's.

I've learned when the enemy attacks, God reacts and goes to work. He knows when you're struggling with a bad medical report or finances or mistreatment. You may not see anything happening, but Almighty God already has the solution. If you will stay in faith, at the right time He will release a flood of His power, a flood of healing, a flood of restoration. He will not only bring you out, He will bring you out better off than you were before.

*"For the LORD your God is the one who goes with you to fight for you against your enemies to give you victory."*

DEUTERONOMY 20:4

## Places of Victory

Remember the place of David's victory "Baal-Perazim—the God of the breakthrough"? Anytime David and his men passed that city they would say, "That's where God released His favor like a flood and gave us a great victory."

God wants us to have our own Baal-Perazims. My mother has her healing of cancer. We have our beautiful Lakewood Church, even though all the experts said we didn't have a chance to get it. We should have places where we can look back and say, "That was where the God of the breakthrough did something amazing in my life. That was where God healed me. That was where God promoted me. That was where God protected me. That was where the God of the breakthrough visited me and my house."

## Great Things

*But thanks be to God! He
gives us the victory through
our Lord Jesus Christ.*

1 CORINTHIANS 15:57

# JANUARY
## 24

Not long ago this lady came up to me so excited. Her family member needed a series of surgeries that were not covered by insurance and were expected to cost $400,000. For months she kept trusting that the God of the breakthrough would make a way. Then, one day out of the blue her employer of nearly thirty years called and said, "You've been so good to our company. We've decided to underwrite the surgeries." The God of the breakthrough released a tidal wave of His favor over her. Now everywhere she goes, she tells everyone what God has done for her family.

He wants to do the same thing for you. He wants to overwhelm you in such a way that everywhere you go you can tell everyone about the great things God has done for you.

## The Promise of Light

*Even in darkness light dawns for the upright, for those who are gracious and compassionate and righteous.*

PSALM 112:4

At times in life it may seem dark. You may not see how it could ever work out. Maybe you don't have the funds to pay your bills. Maybe other problems seem insurmountable. But if you will stay breakthrough-minded, God promises the light will come bursting in as the dawn. That means, suddenly, it will change in your favor. Suddenly, you will catch the break you need. Suddenly, your health turns around. Suddenly, your problems are resolved. Suddenly, a new door opens.

God likes to do things suddenly. When it's dark, don't start complaining. Don't turn negative. Keep reminding yourself that the light is about to come bursting in. It may be today, maybe tomorrow, next week, next month, next year. But know this: Suddenly, things will change in your favor.

## Thinking Too Small

*So do not fear, for I am with you; do not be dismayed, for I am your God. I will strengthen you and help you; I will uphold you with my righteous right hand.*

ISAIAH 41:10

When I'm tempted to think that something will not work out or looks impossible, all I have to do is drive down to our beautiful church in Houston. And I'll think, "God, You did it for us once. I know You can do it for us again."

God wants to release a flood of His power in your life. You may be thinking too small. Maybe you've settled because you think you've reached your limits. No, I can see a tidal wave of God's favor, of promotion, of deliverance, of restoration coming your way. It's the God of the breakthrough releasing His favor like a flood, causing you to overcome obstacles that you thought were insurmountable, causing you to accomplish dreams that you never thought possible.

*"According to your faith let it be done to you."*

## Think Bigger

MATTHEW 9:29

When it comes to our Heavenly Father, don't have a small-minded mentality. Don't have a narrow, limited vision. When you think bigger, God will act bigger. Some people act like they're inconveniencing God. They don't think they can expect their dreams to come to pass. If they can just barely get though life, that's good enough.

Dare to believe. If you think "trickle," you will receive a trickle. If you think "barely get by," you will barely get by. If you think that your problem is too big, it will keep you defeated. But if you will learn to think "flood," you will experience a flood. If you think "overflow," you'll experience an overflow. If you dare think "tidal wave," God can release a tidal wave of His goodness in your life.

## Always Be Ready

*. . . men always ought
to pray and not lose heart.*

LUKE 18:1 NKJV

# JANUARY
# 28

When my father started ministering in small auditoriums and churches back in the 1950s, he carried his sound equipment in the trunk of his car. One night, he accidentally locked his keys in the trunk. No sound equipment meant no service. He and some bystanders tried every trick but couldn't get it open, and time was running out. Then it dawned on him to pray.

When he announced that he was going to pray, the people looked at him like he had lost his mind. But he disregarded the laughter and prayed anyway. When it still would not open, he turned and walked away to more laughter. But all of a sudden they heard this pop. The trunk lid began to rise up toward the heavens, just as if God was saying, "Always be ready. I'm the God of the breakthrough."

## Overtaken

*And all these blessings
shall come upon you and
overtake you if you heed the
voice of the Lord your God.*

DEUTERONOMY 28:2 AMP

You may be accepting things in your life that are far less than God's best. It's been so long you don't see how it could change. Don't ever rule out the God of the breakthrough. Like a flood, His favor can overtake you. Like a flood, God can cause your employer to pay for the surgeries your family member needs. Like a flood, God can cause a trunk to supernaturally pop open. I'm asking you to live breakthrough-minded.

Release your faith in a greater way. If you don't pray for the trunk to open, it won't. Dare to believe. God wants to give you something to talk about. He wants to give you some new Baal-Perazims; new landmarks where you can look back and say, "I know that was the God of the breakthrough."

## Profusely Abounding Favor

*The Spirit of the Lord [is] upon Me, . . .*
*to proclaim the accepted and acceptable year*
*of the Lord [the day when salvation and the*
*free favors of God profusely abound].*

LUKE 4:18–19 AMP

Like Isaiah, I've announced that a flood of God's power is coming. Notice the word used to describe God's favor, *profusely*. That means "overwhelming, out of the norm, exceeding." Favor like you've never seen before. Instead of being overwhelmed by burdens, you will be overwhelmed by God's blessings. But the real question is this: Can you receive this into your spirit?

God works where there is an attitude of faith. Neither the enemy nor other people can stop this flood. You control your own destiny. God is for you. The enemy is against you. You get to cast the deciding vote. I'm asking you to take the limits off of God. He wants to do something new, something amazing in your life. This is the day you will see the free favor of God profusely abound.

## Flooded with Light

*I pray that your hearts will be flooded with light so that you can understand the confident hope he has given to those he called—his holy people who are his rich and glorious inheritance.*

EPHESIANS 1:18 NLT

Paul prayed that the eyes of our understanding would be "flooded with light" so that we would know the amazing future God has in store. Paul experienced a portion of this flood, but this is the day where Paul declared we would see the surpassing greatness of God's favor. Paul was saying in effect, "I've seen one level of God's goodness, but the day we're in, we'll see God's goodness like no generation has seen it before."

I can tell you firsthand, Victoria and I have experienced this flood of God's favor. He has taken us beyond our education, talent, and training and unleashed His abundance, wisdom, and favor in our lives. We have to keep God in first place in our lives. Honor God. Then, learn to take the limits off of Him.

## Like Never Before

*. . . the righteous are as bold as a lion.*

PROVERBS 28:1

My prayer is that you would know how much God loves you, how much He is for you, and what an amazing future He has in store. My prayer is that faith will fill your heart, that you will raise your level of expectancy, and that you will see God's goodness like never before. Because you've been faithful, things have shifted in your favor.

My encouragement for you is for you to wake up every morning and say: "Father, thank You for this flood of favor in my life." Believe big. Pray bold prayers. Then go out expecting favor. If you do that, I believe and declare you will see God's goodness overwhelm you. You are coming into floods of favor, floods of healing, floods of wisdom, floods of good breaks, floods of mercy. Get ready for it.

> *"Look around from where you are, to the north and south, to the east and west. All the land that you see I will give to you and your offspring forever."*

**GENESIS 13:14–15**

### Further Faster

In December 2003, we signed a sixty-year lease with the City of Houston for our Lakewood Church facility. Deep down I knew sometime during that sixty-year period God would give us the ability to purchase the building. Seven years later, the city was running low on funds and asked if we would be interested in purchasing the facility, buying out the lease. A building like ours would cost $400 million to construct. The city did an appraisal, taking into account that any new buyer would still have to honor our sixty-year lease. The appraisal came back not at $100 million, not at $50 million, but at $7.5 million! Today, we own our beautiful facility free and clear.

Here's my point: What could have taken sixty years, God did fifty-three years sooner. He took us further faster, and He can do the same for you.

## Speeding Things Up

*"Before they call I will answer; while they are still speaking I will hear."*

ISAIAH 65:24

# FEBRUARY
# 3

We're living in a day where God is speeding things up. Because you honor God, He will do in a fraction of the time what should have taken you a lifetime to accomplish.

In your career, maybe it should take you twenty years to work your way up to that position, twenty years to build up your business. No, things have shifted. God will give you breaks that you didn't deserve. He will bring the right people across your path. You will see opportunity like you've never seen before. It will take you *further faster*. Get those two words down in your spirit. It may look like in the natural that it will take you years to get out of debt, years to get well, years to overcome that problem. No, you need to get ready. You've come into this shift.

## Acceleration

*"I have seen his ways, and will
heal him; I will also lead him,
and restore comforts to him . . ."*

ISAIAH 57:18 NKJV

Because you've kept God in first place, you
will go further faster, not because you're
working harder, trying to make it all happen. No,
you're putting forth the same effort, being your
best every day, but all of a sudden you get a good
break that thrusts you years down the road. You
get a promotion that you weren't qualified for.

Part of the shift is acceleration. It will not take
as long to accomplish your goals or to get out
of that problem as you think. Almighty God, the
Creator of the universe, is breathing in your direction. He is causing things to fall into place. The
right people will be drawn to you. Good breaks,
opportunities, healing, restoration, favor. It's not
business as usual. You've come into a shift. It will
be business as unusual.

## Keep Hoping

*Let us then approach
God's throne of grace
with confidence, so that
we may receive mercy
and find grace to help us
in our time of need.*

HEBREWS 4:16

I talked to a gentleman who'd had a stroke just a few months before we met. He couldn't move his left arm and had to drag his left leg. The left side of his face was paralyzed. He told me in slurred speech that his doctors estimated that even a partial recovery would take three to five years of therapy, five days a week. They said he'd never be able to lift his left arm.

I told him that God can speed things up. God is in control. I encouraged him to keep believing. Keep hoping. I saw him six months later. The first thing he did was lift his left arm way up in the air and give me a high five. He recovered in less than two months. What happened? God accelerated things.

*Moses answered the people, "Do not be afraid. Stand firm and you will see the deliverance the* LORD *will bring you today."*

EXODUS 14:13

## God Has a Way

You may think it will take you thirty years to pay your house off. You've already run the numbers. No, you don't know what God is up to. You don't know what God has already destined to come across your path. One phone call, one contract, one good break, one inheritance, and you're totally debt free. What should have taken you a lifetime to accomplish, He will do in a split second of time.

Be a believer and not a doubter. You may not see a way, but God still has a way. Your attitude should be: "God, I'm in agreement with You. I believe You have shifted things in my favor. You are taking me further faster. I will accomplish my dreams sooner than I think. I will overcome these problems quicker than I thought."

## The Right People

*In everything he did he had great success,
because the L*ord *was with him.*

1 SAMUEL 18:14

B ack in 1949, a young minister named Billy Graham traveled around the country holding meetings in large auditoriums. He was having success, but he wasn't really nationally known. That summer William Randolph Hearst, who owned newspapers all across the country, heard Graham speak. He was so touched that he sent a message to all of his publishers to write favorable articles about Billy Graham. The next week the whole country was talking about this young minister. Reverend Graham came to national prominence practically overnight because of this one man.

It could have taken Billy Graham his whole lifetime to gain that kind of respect and credibility. Almighty God will open doors that no man can shut. He will connect you to the right people. His favor will thrust you years down the road.

## Open Doors

*"See, I have placed before you an
open door that no one can shut."*

REVELATION 3:8

When William Hearst promoted Billy Graham through his newspapers, what's interesting is he searched out Graham. You don't have to try to find the right people. You just honor God and the right people will find you. They'll pick you out of a crowd. They'll knock on your door. They'll show up at your office. For some reason they will want to be good to you.

God has already lined up the right people for you. It's just a matter of time before they show up. They will open doors that you could not open. They will show you favor even though you didn't ask. They will use their influence to make you look good. They're ordained by God to accelerate His plan for your life and help you go where you could not go on your own.

## A Faster Calculator

*His mother said to the servants, "Do whatever he tells you." . . . They did so, and the master of the banquet tasted the water that had been turned into wine. ". . . you have saved the best till now."*

JOHN 2:5–10

The first miracle Jesus ever performed was when he turned water into wine at the wedding at Cana. To make wine is a very lengthy process. The process from the time they plant the seed to the time they have average-quality wine is typically three to five years. The higher-quality wines take between five and seven years to make. To increase the quality and make it more valuable, often they will age the wine for twenty or thirty years. That would be considered the best wine.

Jesus created fine wine that should have taken twenty years in a split second. In the same way, He can speed up the process of a healing or paying off a home mortgage. The good news is, God has a faster calculator and a much faster schedule.

> *"Look at the nations and watch—and be utterly amazed. For I am going to do something in your days that you would not believe, even if you were told."*

### Utterly Amazing

HABAKKUK 1:5

A woman visited our church while in Houston awaiting a liver transplant at the medical center. Doctors told her she could be on the recipient list between three and five years. She wasn't sure she could make it that long. I encouraged her that God could speed things up. A few weeks later she was back in the church lobby with a real big smile . . . and a new liver. Just two weeks after she was put on the transplant list, a perfectly matched liver for her had become available that wasn't suitable for anyone else on the list.

God took what could have taken years and did it in one month. If you too will take the limits off God, you will see Him do amazing things.

## If You Will Believe

*"The LORD bless you and keep you; the LORD make his face shine on you and be gracious to you . . ."*

NUMBERS 6:24-25

# FEBRUARY
# 11

I have a friend who graduated from college with a big vision to one day lead a major corporation. He went to work for a big company and started in sales. He gave it his best day in and day out, and through successive promotions was appointed vice president at twenty-eight years old. When his boss left, he earned another promotion. The CEO of his corporation was only fifty-one and looked like he had another twenty years in him. But one day, unexpectedly, he resigned and nominated my friend as his successor. Today, at thirty-two years old, he is the youngest CEO in that major corporation's history.

If you will believe and live to honor God, He will let His face shine down on you, and you will accomplish goals in a fraction of the time.

## One Touch of Favor

*I have strength for all things in Christ Who empowers me.*

PHILIPPIANS 4:13 AMP

God put a big dream in the heart of David as a teenager. David knew one day he would accomplish great things. But year after year he was stuck out in the lonely pastures taking care of his father's sheep. I'm sure he felt like he would never get to where God wanted him to be. One day David, knowing the Most High God was with him, faced and defeated the giant Goliath, and in a split second he became a national hero.

One touch of God's favor thrust him years ahead. What's interesting is God used an obstacle to promote David. When you face giant obstacles in your own life—disappointments, setbacks, things don't work out—don't become discouraged. That adversity could be where you see God speed up the time and you accomplish something that should have taken your whole lifetime.

## Divine Connections

*At this, she bowed down with her face to the ground. She asked him, "Why have I found such favor in your eyes that you notice me—a foreigner?"*

RUTH 2:10

Our friends Jerry and Jana Lackey moved to rural Botswana, Africa, to take care of orphans, feed the poor, and teach people. Their big dream, however, was to build a major youth center, but it was estimated to cost $5 million— what seemed a lifetime's worth of fundraising. Then one day a German businessman was visiting Botswana with his wife, and they fell in love with the country. Wanting to do something to help, they Googled the phrase "Botswana orphanages," and the Lackey's organization came up. What started with a $20,000 donation was followed by $300,000, then the purchase of an exclusive safari resort and the writing of a check for $5 million! On April 4, 2013, our friends dedicated that brand new youth center, totally paid for by their German benefactor.

God brought one man across their paths, a divine connection.

*How great are his signs,
how mighty his wonders! His
kingdom is an eternal kingdom;
his dominion endures from
generation to generation.*

DANIEL 4:3

## Agree with God

If you want to see a shift occur in your own life, you cannot harbor thoughts of defeat and lack and mediocrity. You've must get in agreement and say, "Yes, God. This is for me. I believe You have lined up the right people. I know they're already in my future. I want to thank You that I will accomplish my dreams sooner than I think."

In the natural it may not look like it, but remember, we serve a supernatural God. He is about to release floods of His favor, floods of healing, floods of good breaks. Take the limits off God. Don't think of all the reasons your plans won't work. God wouldn't have given you the dream unless He already had a way to bring it to pass. That's the way our God is.

## Strong Roots

*"It was majestic in beauty, with its spreading boughs, for its roots went down to abundant waters."*

EZEKIEL 31:7

# FEBRUARY
# 15

I read that the Chinese bamboo plant barely grows aboveground for its first four years. While you hardly see anything happening, under the ground it's developing a massive root system spreading out in every possible direction. In the fifth year, once the roots are properly established, the plant will suddenly shoot up to as high as eighty feet in the air—all in one year.

You have been faithful, given, served, and helped others. You've sown a lot of seeds, but you haven't seen a lot of progress. So far, you've lived the equivalent of your four years of developing roots. You were proving to God that you would be faithful. Now God is saying, "You're coming into your fifth year. You will see explosive growth that will take you to levels beyond your income, beyond your training, beyond your experience."

## Stress Lifter

*Cast your burden on the LORD, and He shall sustain you; He shall never permit the righteous to be moved.*

PSALM 55:22 NKJV

I have a good friend who had been caught in a difficult legal situation for at least a year. It had been very heavy on her heart. She was told her opponents could drag it out for ten years to resolve just to make her life miserable. Facing years and years of this stress and frustration, she was like a different person: no joy, no peace, no victory, very solemn, very serious. But a week ago as I write this, she received the good news that the case was totally resolved in her favor. Everything was cleared up. She said, "Joel, I can't even tell you what a load is being lifted off of me."

What could have taken ten years, God resolved in less than a year. God will cause things to fall into place.

## Favor Time

*God is not unjust; he will not forget your work
and the love you have shown him as you have helped
his people and continue to help them.*

HEBREWS 6:10

The Scripture talks about how God will reward us in this life, not just in the Sweet By and By. Because you've been faithful, you will reap from all the seeds you've sown down through the years. Nothing you've ever given has gone unnoticed. Every sacrifice you've made, every time you stopped to help someone, God sees that. He is about to release everything that belongs to you. It's favor time.

You will soon see acceleration. The right people will search you out. Opportunity will come knocking on your door. God will bring out gifts and talents you didn't even know you had. It will not take a lifetime to accomplish your dreams. It will happen in a fraction of the time. It will happen sooner than you think. It will be bigger than you imagined.

## Mountains into Roads

*"I will turn all my mountains into roads,*
*and my highways will be raised up."*

ISAIAH 49:11

I was driving through the mountains not long ago, and on one side there was a huge wall of rock where the road had been cut into the mountainside. The builders had used dynamite to blast away the rock; otherwise, the stone would have been there probably forever.

We all have things in our lives that seem permanent. Maybe it looks like you will never get out of debt, or like you will stay at the same earning level the rest of your life. But just as the builders used dynamite to blast away the rock so they could create that mountain road, God has explosive blessings that will remove obstacles that may look permanent now. One touch of God's favor can blast you out of debt. One good break can blast you to a new level.

## His Ear to Hear

> LORD, *You have heard the desire of the humble; You will prepare their heart; You will cause Your ear to hear . . .*
>
> PSALM 10:17 NKJV

A friend of mine wanted to go to a certain college but he needed a scholarship. Although his grades were good enough, the college informed him there were no more scholarships available. At that point, he didn't have the funds, so he enrolled in a junior college. All the facts said his dream of going to his favorite college was permanently over. But four weeks before school was to start, this college called back and said a scholarship had opened up. Instead of the two-year partial scholarship he had applied for earlier, they offered him a four-year full ride. Now when he graduates, instead of owing thousands of dollars, he'll be debt free. That is an explosive blessing.

God has a way of removing what looks permanent by showing us an explosion of His goodness.

*Enlarge the place of your tent,
and let the curtains of your
habitations be stretched out;
spare not; lengthen your cords
and strengthen your stakes, for
you will spread abroad to the
right hand and to the left.*

ISAIAH 54:2–3 AMP

## Sudden, Widespread Increase

You may think your current situation is permanent. You've been there a long time, and you can't see how you could ever move up. All the facts are telling you it's impossible that things will improve, but God has ways to increase you that you've never dreamed of. He's saying today: "You need to get ready. I have explosive blessings coming your way. I will take you higher. I will increase you beyond your income. I will suddenly change things for the better in your life."

One definition of the word *explosion* is "a sudden, widespread increase." That's what God will do for you. Suddenly, you're not expecting anything. It's out of the ordinary. It's not small. It's not mediocre. It's a widespread increase. It's so amazing you'll know it's the hand of God.

## Abundant Blessings

*And I will make of you a great nation, and I will bless you [with abundant increase of favors] and make your name famous and distinguished, and you will be a blessing [dispensing good to others].*

GENESIS 12:2 AMP

A gentleman stopped by Lakewood Church recently and brought a very large donation to the ministry. It was his tithe. He said he'd received an inheritance from a relative he'd never met. He didn't even know they were related, but this man left him a gift that thrust his family to a whole new level financially. He not only paid off his own home loan but also paid off the mortgages held by some other people.

You may feel that in the natural you could never accomplish your dreams. You don't have the connections, the resources, or the education, but God is saying: "You have not seen My explosive blessings. You haven't seen the surpassing greatness of My favor. I have blessings that will catapult you years ahead. I have increase beyond your calculations."

## Deserts into Pools

*"I, the God of Israel, will . . .
make rivers flow on barren
heights, and springs within
the valleys. I will turn the desert
into pools of water, and the
parched ground into springs."*

ISAIAH 41:17–18

I've learned God doesn't always take us ahead in normal increments. There are times where God takes us little by little. We have to be faithful day in and day out, but when you hit an explosive blessing instead of moving up from seven to eight you'll go from seven to thirty-four. That's widespread increase.

The good news is the economy is not our source. God is our source. The economy in Heaven is doing just fine. As long as we stay connected to the vine, putting our trust in Him, you and I are connected to a supply line that will never run dry. Release your faith for explosive blessings. Believe that you can break out of what's holding you back and become everything God created you to be. Incredible power is released when we believe.

## Hidden Treasures

*"I will give you hidden treasures, riches stored in secret places, so that you may know that I am the LORD, the God of Israel, who summons you by name."*

ISAIAH 45:3

I heard about a married couple who wanted to buy a house in a prestigious neighborhood but didn't feel at peace when they went to move forward. Instead, they purchased a property just outside the subdivision. About six months later, an oil company told them they had discovered oil under the whole subdivision, but that property was too densely populated to drill in. The oil company leased part of this couple's property, giving them a commission from their property as well as a portion of the commissions from all the 1,200 homes in the subdivision!

God knows where the treasures are! He knows the inventions that have not yet been created, the ideas that will be successful, and the properties that will be valuable. He leads you to that one idea that will catapult you to a new level.

*By faith Abraham, when called to go to a place he would later receive as his inheritance, obeyed and went, even though he did not know where he was going.*

HEBREWS 11:8

## Out of the Rut

In 1946, Truett Cathy and his brother opened a little restaurant, the Dwarf Grill, south of downtown Atlanta. Although hamburgers were the rage, God gave him an idea that if people like hamburgers, maybe they'd like chicken sandwiches, too. So he started to offer boneless chicken breast sandwiches to his customers, too. They were so popular, he opened his first shopping mall fast food restaurant in 1967 and called it Chick-fil-A. Today, there are more than 1,700 Chick-fil-As in thirty-nine states. The Cathys give millions of dollars to help people around the world—an explosive blessing.

God has new inventions, new businesses, new books, new technology, new medicine, and new procedures just waiting to be released. Get out of a rut, enlarge your vision, and start thanking God for the explosive blessings coming your way.

## Reign in Life

*. . . how much more will those who receive God's*
*abundant provision of grace and of the gift of righteousness*
*reign in life through the one man, Jesus Christ!*

ROMANS 5:17

Lakewood Church is a $400 million facility that we bought for about $20 million. After we renovated it, our investment was still less than a fourth of what it would have cost new. We saw the exceeding greatness of God's favor move us from inadequate facilities to the premier facility in the fourth largest city in America. That's what God is doing today. He's stepping it up a notch. We were never created to be second class and just barely get by. The Scripture says we are supposed to reign in life as kings.

Don't settle where you are. Make room for explosive blessings in your thinking. He's about to release buildings, contracts, ideas, favor, influence that will catapult His people to new levels. Get ready for God to open up doors wider than you thought possible.

## Stand Out

*"'Well done, my good servant!' his master replied.
'Because you have been trustworthy in a very small matter,
take charge of ten cities.'"*

LUKE 19:17

A friend of mine started his business with just one employee—himself. Within a few years his business occupied a whole floor in a downtown high-rise. Recently he was awarded a multi-billion-dollar contract to build one of the largest refineries in all of China. The competition included much larger companies that had been in business for decades, but God caused both him and his company to stand out. This is part of the shift of wealth to God's people, who will further the Kingdom.

God will cause you to stand out just like my friend. You may seem the least likely for a promotion in the natural, but with the blessing of God on your life, the odds dramatically change. You and God are a majority. Get ready for an explosion of God's goodness, a sudden, widespread increase.

## Laid Up for You

*. . . the wealth of the sinner [finds its way eventually] into the hands of the righteous, for whom it was laid up.*

PROVERBS 13:22 AMP

God has already stored up businesses, contracts, buildings, increase, promotions, and ideas. They already have your name on them, and if you'll just keep being your best, blessing others, honoring God, and dreaming big, eventually they will find their way into your hands, the hands of the righteous. God says the wealth of the ungodly will eventually find its way into the hands of the godly.

The building where our church is located was called the Summit at first, and then later the Compaq Center. But I believe if you peeled those names back thirty years ago when it was first built, the name Lakewood Church was already there. The stadium eventually found its way into our hands. You don't know the amazing things that God has already put your name on. They're already laid up for you.

*To the person who pleases him, God gives wisdom, knowledge and happiness, but to the sinner he gives the task of gathering and storing up wealth to hand it over to the one who pleases God.*

ECCLESIASTES 2:26

## "Eventually"s

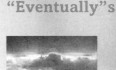

God is saying: "I'm shifting things from the hands of those who are not concerned about Me, from those who don't walk in integrity to the hands of people I can trust with furthering My Kingdom." Somebody else may have started them, but God says eventually they will find the way into your hands. You have some "eventually"s in your future. You know what an "eventually" is? It's an explosive blessing: Unexpectedly a business, a real estate deal, an extraordinary contract, or an inheritance falls into your hands that could only be God's doing.

I'm asking you to believe that God has amazing things in store. Believe that you can break out of what's holding you back and become everything God created you to be. Incredible power is released when we believe.

# The Lord's Goodness

*[What, what would have become of me] had I not believed that I would see the Lord's goodness in the land of the living!*

FEBRUARY

## 29

PSALM 27:13 AMP

On Mother's Day 2009, a couple who had tried everything medically to have a baby for six years came to a Lakewood service. I talked about how everything that has our name on it is coming back in. I said specifically, "The baby who has your name is coming in." The couple instantly received this as God's promise for them and released their faith. They left the service knowing that the baby with their name was coming in. Four hours later, as they were celebrating Mother's Day with their family, their office manager called and asked if they would be interested in adopting a baby boy to be born in July. They knew that was the hand of God. Eight weeks later they put their arms around their son.

The release of our faith works wonders.

## Get in Agreement

*"If you do not stand firm in your faith, you will not stand at all."*

ISAIAH 7:9

What is the key that allows God to do great things? The only promises that will come alive in your life and end up becoming realities are the promises where you rise up and say, "Yes, that's for me." You have to get in agreement with God and let it take root.

I can speak faith and victory over your future, but if you make excuses and talk yourself out of it, that promise will not take root. But when the soil of your heart is fertile, you have expectancy in your spirit. If you hear the promise that God has blessings in your future, you'll rise up and say, "That's for me. Lord, I believe. I release my faith for explosive blessings, for the immeasurable, limitless, surpassing greatness of Your favor."

## The Shift

*"Your gates will always
stand open, they will never
be shut, day or night, so that
people may bring you the
wealth of the nations . . ."*

ISAIAH 60:11

A pastor friend of mine was planning to build a $40 million sanctuary. One day, out of the blue, the mayor called and said the developers of a huge casino near his church had gone bankrupt before finishing it. The completed building would be much bigger and better than his planned facility, and it was for sale—not for $50 million or more but for under $2 million. Then the owner of a production company heard about the possible building sale and offered to sell them a 150 foot-long screen used for concerts and sporting events that cost $3 million new for $50,000. Everything fell into place!

That's a part of the shift, the transfer. Somebody else built it, somebody else paid for it, but at the right time the building found its way into the hands of the godly.

*Take delight in the LORD,*
*and he will give you the*
*desires of your heart.*

PSALM 37:4

## Desires of Your Heart

I'm convinced there are times when we don't see God's amazing hand at work, because we don't activate our faith by believing. We think of all the reasons why it won't happen. I'm asking you to let this seed take root. God has explosive blessings in your future. He is about to release another level of His favor in your life. He is going to give you the desires of your heart.

This is the generation for the surpassing greatness of God's favor. Things you've been praying about for years are about to come to pass. Situations that have been stuck for a long time are about to break loose. It will not happen in an ordinary way or the way you had planned. God will do it in an extraordinary way so you know it's His doing.

## Enlarge Your Vision

*Be strong and take heart,*
*all you who hope in the LORD.*

PSALM 31:24

# MARCH
# 4

Even though God has amazing things in your future, He is limited by your capacity to receive. It's as if you have a one-gallon bucket, yet He has fifty gallons to give you. The problem is not with the supply but with your capacity to receive.

If you think you've reached your limits—whether it's because of a bad economy, your health is poor, or you can't afford the house you want—God has the ability and resources to help you, but your container is too small. You can't go around thinking thoughts of mediocrity and expect to excel. You can't think thoughts of lack and expect to have abundance. The two don't go together. You have to enlarge your vision and make room for the new things God wants to do.

## Something Bigger

*. . . when you open your
hand, they are satisfied
with good things.*

PSALM 104:28

Some people go around with a small cup, so to speak. They're not expecting much; maybe it's because they've struggled for many years. Others may have a bucket instead of a cup. They've done okay, but they're not planning on going any further. Still others have stretched their faith and have a barrel. They believe they will go higher.

If you trade in that small container and get something bigger, God can give you more. Your attitude should be: "The economy may be down, but I know God is still on the Throne. I know He has promotion and increase already lined up for me. His favor surrounds me like a shield. Goodness and mercy are following me. This will be a great year." When you change your thinking like that, you enlarge your capacity to receive.

## According to Your Faith

*Now to him who is able to do immeasurably
more than all we ask or imagine, according
to his power that is at work within us . . .*

EPHESIANS 3:20

Some people go through life with a cup, others have a bucket, and some have a barrel. Yet there's one other group. They believe in far-and-beyond favor. They believe God will prosper them even in a recession. They believe their children will be mighty in the land. They're expecting explosive blessings and unprecedented favor. They know they've come into a shift and a supernatural increase is coming. Their faith is so strong they have a barn.

Jesus said, "According to your faith, it will be done unto you." He was saying in effect, "If you have a cup, I'll fill you with a cupful of blessings. If you have a barrel, I'll fill you with a barrelful of blessings. But if you have a barn, I will give you a barnful of blessings."

## Open Up

*"I am the LORD your God . . .*
*Open wide your mouth and I will fill it."*

PSALM 81:10

My question is this: Do you have your mouth opened wide? What are you expecting? What are you saying about your future? If you're thinking about how tough a year it is, that you'll never get promoted or ever get well, then your mouth is barely open. You're not expecting increase. You're not expecting good breaks. You're not expecting God to turn it around.

When you have your mouth opened wide, you're expecting to have a blessed year. You're praying not only that your children turn around but that God makes your children mighty in the land. You're not just believing you will make the monthly mortgage payments but that you will pay off your whole house. If you'll take the limits off God—if you'll get up every morning expecting far-and-beyond favor—He won't disappoint you.

## Don't Settle

*You have dwelt long enough on this mountain. . . . Behold, I have set the land before you; go in and take possession of the land which the Lord swore to your fathers . . .*

DEUTERONOMY 1:6, 8 AMP

When the children of Israel were headed toward the Promised Land, they had big dreams and big goals, but along the way they faced adversities. They had some disappointments. They were like many modern-day people who lost money when the stock market dropped or lost their homes when the recession hit. The children of Israel became so discouraged they gave up on their dreams and just settled where they were.

One day God told them they had been there long enough. I believe God is saying that to each one of us. You may have dreamed big, but after some setbacks you just settled for the status quo. God is saying to you, "This is a new day. Get your fire back. Where you are is not where you're supposed to stay."

*And my God will meet all your needs according to the riches of his glory in Christ Jesus.*

PHILIPPIANS 4:19

## Give God Permission

God brought things across my path years ago, but I turned them down. I thought they were too big. I didn't think I was qualified. It was so far beyond what I thought I could handle, I didn't release my faith for it. I wasn't giving God permission to increase me. I missed that opportunity to go farther. God will not force us to live His abundant life.

I'm asking you to increase your capacity to receive. You may have been living out your life the same as how you were raised and that's all you've ever known. Stretch your faith and dream bigger. Go beyond the barriers that have held you back. Make room for God to do something new. Give Him permission to increase you. You have to give God permission to prosper you.

## New Wineskins

*"And no one pours new wine into old wineskins. Otherwise, the wine will burst the skins, and both the wine and the wineskins will be ruined. No, they pour new wine into new wineskins."*

MARCH

# 10

MARK 2:22

When Jesus referred to pouring new wine into old wineskins, He meant that you can't go to a new level with an old way of thinking. You may be ready for God to do something new. When you hear that God has more in store, something on the inside says, "Yes, this is for me." But many times your mind will come up with reasons why it's not going to happen—the bad economy, a negative report from the doctor, etc.

No, get rid of the old wineskins. Trade in those containers for something new and bigger. What's happened in the past is over and done. Have a bigger vision for your life. Our attitude should be: "This is my year to go to a new level. This is my year to see a supernatural increase."

## "Borrow Not a Few"

*Then he said, Go around and
borrow vessels from all your
neighbors, empty vessels—and
not a few. And when you come
in, . . . pour out [the oil you have]
into all those vessels, setting aside
each one when it is full.*

2 KINGS 4:3–4 AMP

In 2 Kings 4, there's a story of a widow who has
no money to pay her bills. The creditors are
coming to take her sons as payment. Elisha the
Prophet tells her to go to her neighbors and borrow as many big empty pots as possible—specifically, "Borrow not a few." He was saying, "Don't
shortchange yourself. Make room for abundance."

When she returned with her borrowed pots,
Elisha told her to pour the little oil that she had
into one of those empty containers. It looked as
if she was just transferring it from one to another,
but the Scripture says the oil never ran out. She
kept pouring and pouring. God supernaturally
multiplied that oil until every one of those containers was completely full. That is the far-and-
beyond favor of God.

## Unlimited Supplies

> *When all the jars were full, she said to her son, "Bring me another one." But he replied, "There is not a jar left." Then the oil stopped flowing.*

2 KINGS 4:6

Did you notice that whether the widow borrowed one or ten or fifty containers, they would have been full? The amount of increase she received wasn't up to God. He has unlimited supplies. It was up to her. That was why the prophet said, "Borrow not a few."

My question is: How many containers are you borrowing? What kind of vision do you have for your life? If you think, "The economy is so bad, and I'm just hoping to survive," God says, "All right, I'll fill that barely-get-by container." Or maybe you believe you can pay your bills, feed your family, and have a little left over. That's good. God will fill those containers. But I believe you are different. You have radical faith. You're calling Home Depot to say: "I need a couple thousand empty containers."

*"For I know the plans I have for you,"* declares the LORD, *"plans to prosper you and not to harm you, plans to give you hope and a future."*

JEREMIAH 29:11

## More Than Enough

Like the widow woman and the pots of cooking oil, God wants to bless you beyond your normal income, beyond your salary, and beyond your retirement. He can do exceedingly abundantly above and beyond. He is El Shaddai, the God who is more than enough. God is saying, "You need to get ready. I'm going to fill your containers." It may not have happened yet, but God has favor in your future.

You're positioned under the open windows of Heaven. You may not see how it can happen, but God has ways to increase you that you've never thought of. Make room for this far-and-beyond favor. God has explosive blessings that can thrust you to a new level. He can give you one good break; one promotion, one inheritance, and all those containers will be filled to overflowing.

## Rise Higher

*Surely the arm of the LORD is not too short to save,
nor his ear too dull to hear.*

ISAIAH 59:1

Don't go around year after year expecting the same thing the same way. God is a God of increase. He has greater levels. Where you are is not where you're supposed to stay. You're supposed to rise higher. Have a bigger vision. Not, "God, if You'll just give me this small raise, I'll be happy. God, if You'll just help my car to not break down. God, if You'll just help me to scrape by, You know how bad the economy is."

Don't shortchange yourself. God is saying to you: "Don't limit your vision. Don't limit what I can do for you." You may not see how it could happen. That's okay; that's not your job. Your job is to believe. God has a thousand ways to fill your life with blessings that you've never thought of.

## Big Fish

*On this mountain the LORD Almighty will prepare*
*a feast of rich food for all peoples, a banquet of aged wine—*
*the best of meats and the finest of wines.*

ISAIAH 25:6

A fisherman was on a riverbank one day when he noticed another man fishing nearby who threw back every big fish he caught but kept every small fish he hooked. When his curiosity peaked, he finally went over and asked him why he'd thrown the big fish back. "Oh, that's simple," said the other man. "All I have is a ten-inch frying pan."

There are a lot of people like that. Instead of making room for increase and believing for great things, they go around with an attitude that says, "I could never live in that neighborhood. I could never afford that college. I'll never be that successful. We're just ten-inch frying-pan people." God has some big fish in your future. Do yourself a favor and get rid of that ten-inch frying-pan mentality.

## To the Top

*The LORD will make you the head, not the tail. If you pay attention to the commands of the LORD your God that I give you this day and carefully follow them, you will always be at the top, never at the bottom.*

DEUTERONOMY 28:13

My father was raised in poverty, lack, and defeat. In high school, he was given the Christmas basket donated for the poorest family. All they could afford to drink was something called "Blue John" milk that was usually fed only to the hogs. Every circumstance said he was stuck there. But at seventeen years old, he gave his life to Christ and something rose up inside of him—a faith, a boldness—that said, "My children will never be raised in the poverty and defeat I was raised in." He took the limits off God and went on to live a blessed, abundant life.

No matter how you were raised or what has pushed you down or held you back, God is saying, "I created you as the head and not the tail. I made you to lend and not borrow."

*Surely your goodness*
*and love will follow me*
*all the days of my life . . .*

PSALM 23:6

## Who Says?

I read about a young man who bought a fifty-acre plot of land from his great-aunt so she could afford to move into a senior's home. He paid $1,000 an acre—$50,000 for the land—but it wasn't worth that much. He did it just to help out his family member. However, a surveyor discovered that right under the surface of the property was Goshen stone—some of the most beautiful and sought-after landscaping stone around. Geologists estimated there were twenty-four million tons of this stone on his property. It sells for about $100 a ton, which means the stone on his land was worth more than $2 billion!

Who says you'll never own a nice home? Who says you'll never take a mission trip? Who says you'll never send your children to college? All it takes is one touch of God's favor.

# In One Day

*With the Lord a day is like a thousand years, and a thousand years are like a day.*

2 PETER 3:8

## MARCH
# 18

If you'll stay in faith, God can take a thousand years of blessings and release them in one day. Dare to say, "God, I'm asking you to give me the blessings that my ancestors missed out on." That may seem far out, but we serve a far-out God. What He has planned for your future is more than you can imagine.

If you open your mouth wide, God will fill it. Get rid of the cup, get rid of the bucket, and get rid of the barrel. God has a barn load of blessings stored up for you. Don't let a limited mindset hold you back. If you'll take off the limits and make room for Him to do something new, you'll go beyond the barriers of the past and step into the abundance God has in store.

## Unshakable Confidence

**MARCH**

# 19

*But none of these things move me . . .*

ACTS 20:24 AMP

When God puts a promise in your heart, you have to come to the place, as the Apostle Paul did, where you believe in that promise so strongly no one can talk you out of it. All the circumstances may indicate you'll never get well, never get out of debt, never accomplish your dreams, never meet the right person, or never see your family restored. But deep down you've got to have this confidence—a knowing that God is still on the Throne.

He is bigger than any obstacle. He already has a way. He is working behind the scenes. What He promised will come to pass at the right time. You don't get discouraged if it takes a long time. You don't complain if there is a setback. You have this unshakable confidence.

## Live in Peace

> *For as many as are the promises of God, they all find their Yes [answer] in Him [Christ].*
>
> 2 CORINTHIANS 1:20 AMP

Circumstances can look impossible. People may say it will never happen. But your attitude needs to be: "It doesn't change my mind. I'm not moved by what I see, whether it's a medical report, the economy, my job situation, or how my children are acting. I am moved by what I know. And I know if God is for me, who dares be against me? I know all of God's promises are yes and amen. I know God has the final say."

That's an unshakable faith. You're not moved by the circumstances. You are not up when something good happens and down when you don't see anything happening. You know everything God promised you is in your future. So you live in peace. You are not upset, frustrated, or discouraged. You are content.

> *Yet [Abraham] did not waver through unbelief regarding the promise of God, but was strengthened in his faith and gave glory to God, being fully persuaded that God had power to do what he had promised.*
>
> ROMANS 4:20–21

## Unwavering

God gave Abraham a promise that his wife would have a child. In the natural, childbirth was impossible for them. Abraham and his wife Sarah were each nearly a hundred years old. How could Abraham have this unwavering faith when in the natural all the odds were against him? It says, "He did not consider his own body, already dead . . . , and the deadness of Sarah's womb" (Romans 4:19 NKJV). The key to having unshakable faith is to not consider your circumstances, but consider your God.

If you consider only the negatives, doubt will creep in, keeping you from God's best. But when you know God is on the Throne working on your behalf, you go out each day with passion, with expectancy, and looking for the great things God has in store.

## God's Law Supersedes

*So we say with confidence,
"The Lord is my helper;
I will not be afraid. What
can mere mortals do to me?"*

MARCH

# 22

HEBREWS 13:6

Recently we were on our way to an event and stopped dead in a traffic jam. One member of our group called ahead and informed those waiting for us that we would be late. They sent a police escort to bring us in, and one of the officers actually drove our car. He drove us around the stalled traffic and then fifteen miles over the speed limit to get us there. We could break the law because the law was driving us.

You can benefit in the same way. In the natural, your circumstance may be impossible. But the good news is Someone who is riding with you supersedes those laws. God's law supersedes the laws of medicine, the laws of science, and the laws of finance. When you focus on God instead of on your circumstances, amazing things can happen.

## More Than Facts

*"'But I will restore you to health and heal your wounds,' declares the LORD . . ."*

JEREMIAH 30:17

Too often we consider only what we can see and only where we are right now. We analyze and do projections based only upon the cold hard facts. But there are times when every circumstance and every report says, "It's impossible," and we have to determine to focus on God and His power to supersede all things in the natural.

The economy may be down, but God says He will prosper you even in the desert. Your checkbook may say you will not make the mortgage payment, but God says He will supply all of your needs. It may seem like you will never get out of debt, but God says, "You will lend and not borrow." Your medical report may say your only option is to live with that sickness, but God says, "I will restore health unto you."

## "The Great I Am"

*God said to Moses, "I AM WHO I AM.*
*This is what you are to say to the Israelites:*
*'I AM has sent me to you.'"*

EXODUS 3:14

When you focus only on feelings of discouragement and loneliness, you may not be able to foresee anything good happening in your life. But when you consider God, you realize your best days are ahead. Your future will be brighter than your past. The greatest victories are not behind you; they are in front of you.

Are you considering your circumstances? Or are you considering your God and His power to supersede all things in the natural? He is called "the Great I Am." He's saying, "I am everything you need. If you're sick, I'm your healer. If you're struggling, I'm your provider. If you're worried, I'm your peace. If you're lonely, I'm your friend. If you're in trouble, I'm your deliverer. If you need a break, I'm your favor."

## If God Wants

*"Is anything too hard for the Lord?"*

GENESIS 18:14

My friend Courtney applied for a scholarship at a major university. Twenty-six hundred students applied for only twelve scholarships. She could have thought, "What's the use? Those are terrible odds. Less than half of one percent." But her attitude was: "God, you control the whole universe, and if You want me in this college, I believe You will cause me to stand out. I'm not moved by what I see; I'm moved by what I know. I know Your plans for me are for good. I know You have far-and-beyond favor. I know You reward those who honor You."

A few months ago, Courtney was notified that she was one of the twelve chosen for a full scholarship. When you consider God and not your circumstances, God will show up and do amazing things.

## All Your Needs

> *"When I broke the five loaves for the five thousand, how many basketfuls of pieces did you pick up?"* *"Twelve,"* they replied.
>
> MARK 8:19

When we acquired the Compaq Center for Lakewood Church, our architects said the renovations would cost about $100 million. After our financial team ran the numbers, we realized we couldn't make it work on paper. After I analyzed the facts a hundred different ways, I did what I'm asking you to do: I said, "God, I'm changing my focus. You took five loaves and fed five thousand. And You gave us this beautiful building when all the odds were against us. You said You would supply our needs according to Your riches."

When I focused on God, faith and hope rose up. I became fully persuaded that He would make a way, even though I didn't see a way. Today, all of us at Lakewood Church are not just dreaming the dream; we also are living the dream in our beautiful facility.

*"Do you have eyes but fail to see, and ears but fail to hear? And don't you remember?"*

MARK 8:18

## Consider God

What you focus on in life is so important. What are you dwelling on right now? Is it the size of the obstacle, or the size of your God? If you go around all day thinking about your problems, worried, anxious, and playing all the negative scenarios in your mind, you will draw in the negative. You're using your faith, but you're using it in reverse. It takes the same amount of energy to be negative and worry as it does to be positive and to believe. I'm asking you to use your energy for the right purposes.

Most people have considered their difficult circumstances long enough. They've considered the medical report, the bank statement, and the odds against them over and over. Now it's time to make a switch and start considering God.

# Magnify God

*Now thanks be to God who always leads us in triumph in Christ, and through us diffuses the fragrance of His knowledge in every place.*

2 CORINTHIANS 2:14 NKJV

Why don't you spend the same time you would normally be worrying about problems to thanking God for the answers that are on the way. Instead of overanalyzing a bad situation, spend your time meditating on the Scripture. Instead of reading the bad medical report for the twelve hundredth time, go walk in the park and with every step say: "Lord, thank You that You're still on the Throne. You have me in the palm of Your hand, and nothing can snatch me away."

Here's a key: When you make God bigger, your problems become smaller. When you magnify God instead of magnifying your difficulties, faith rises in your heart. That faith will keep you fully persuaded. Pay attention to what you focus on. Be aware of what's playing in your mind all day. Consider your God.

## Believe
## God's Report

MARCH

29

*While Jesus was still speaking,*
*some people came from the*
*house of Jairus, the synagogue*
*leader. "Your daughter is dead,"*
*they said. "Why bother the*
*teacher anymore?"*

MARK 5:35

When Jesus heard the report that the sick girl He was on His way to pray for had died, He said, "Don't be afraid; just believe" (Mark 5:36). Sometimes in order to stay in faith you have to ignore a negative report. It doesn't mean you deny the facts and act like they are not there. Instead, just like Jesus, you choose not to dwell on it. God has another report.

Whose report will you believe? God says, "Whatever you touch will prosper and succeed. You will lend and not borrow." Get in agreement with God. Other reports may say, "You'll never accomplish your dreams. You'll never meet the right person. You'll never get that promotion." God's report says, "Because you delight yourself in Me, I will give you the desires of your heart."

## All Things Are Possible

*Jesus looked at them and said, "With man this is impossible, but with God all things are possible."*

MATTHEW 19:26

A lady once told me that she had a rare form of cancer and a very short life expectancy. Even though I'd just talked about someone beating cancer three times, she had no hope. She told me detail after detail of why she couldn't get well. She had analyzed it and reanalyzed it. By the time she finished, she had convinced me. No wonder she didn't have faith.

It's good to have information. You shouldn't live with your head in the sand, but at some point you have to say, "I want to know the facts, but I don't need to know all the details of why I will not get well, or why I'll never be debt free, or why I'll never accomplish my dreams." If you don't cut off negative information, it will depress you. Step out of the natural and say, "This may be impossible with men, but I know with God all things are possible."

> *[Jesus] said to Simon, "Put out into deep water, and let down the nets for a catch." Simon answered, "Master, we've worked hard all night and haven't caught anything. But because you say so, I will let down the nets."*

## If Jesus Says So

LUKE 5:4–6

The fisherman could have said to Jesus, "We appreciate your advice, but we're the experts, and the fish are not there." It's so easy for our intellects to get in the way of what God wants to do. But Jesus finally convinced them, "What I've promised you may not make sense in the natural, but I have supernatural power." It did not seem logical, but they were rewarded with so many fish their nets were breaking.

Make sure you don't talk yourself out of what God wants to do in your life. All your reasoning may say it will never happen. It may seem that the report is too bad and all the odds are against you. But dare to do what the doubt-filled fishermen did and say, "Nevertheless, if You say so, I believe so."

## According to His Word

*But the angel said to her, "Do not be afraid, Mary;
you have found favor with God. You will conceive and
give birth to a son, and you are to call him Jesus."*

LUKE 1:30–31

God spoke an incredible promise to Mary, who was only a teenager at the time. You can imagine the doubts that bombarded her: "You can't have a child without a man. That defies the laws of nature." If Mary had only looked at what was possible in the natural, she would have given up. But Mary didn't consider her circumstances. She considered her God.

I love the way she replied to the angel. "Be it unto me according to your word." Mary was saying, "If God says the impossible can happen, I believe the impossible will happen. I will not talk myself out of it. I believe." When God puts a promise in our hearts, we may not understand how something can happen, but we don't reason it out. We become fully persuaded.

## Not Dependent on Man

*Then Mary said to the angel, "How can this be,*
*since I do not know a man?"*

LUKE 1:34 NKJV

When the angel told Mary she would give birth to Jesus, she asked how that could be possible, since she had never been with a man. She was talking about the physical, but I believe God was saying, "My promises are not dependent on man." You don't have to have a certain person to fulfill your destiny or your boss to give you a promotion. God's promises are not dependent on who you know or who you don't know. The main thing is for you to know Him. God controls it all.

The Scripture says promotion doesn't come from people, it comes from God (Psalm 75:5–7). When it's your time to be promoted or healed or restored, God doesn't check with your friends, your boss, or your family. As the angel told Mary, God will make it happen without a man.

**Everything You Need**

| *Surely, LORD, you bless the righteous; you surround them with your favor as with a shield.*

PSALM 5:12

It's easy to focus on what we don't have—the talent, the education, or the personality. But as long as you think you're lacking, it will keep you from God's best. It's important to have faith in God, but you should also have faith in what God has given you. You are equipped, empowered, and have the talent, the resources, the personality, everything you need to fulfill your destiny.

Here's the key: You have exactly what you need. If you will use what God has given you, He will get you to where you're supposed to be. It's not necessarily the amount of talent, education, or money. What makes the difference is God's anointing on your life. You can have average talent, but when God breathes in your direction, you'll go further than someone with exceptional talent.

*Finding a fresh jawbone
of a donkey, [Samson]
grabbed it and struck down
a thousand men.*

JUDGES 15:15

## Ordinary to Extraordinary

You can have an extraordinary problem, but with the favor of God, He can provide an ordinary solution and make you victorious. That's what happened with Samson when a huge army surrounded him. He had no weapons, no protection. All he could find was the jawbone of a donkey. It was small and ordinary, but Samson realized that this jawbone was part of his divine destiny. Even though that jawbone was ordinary, it became extraordinary when God breathed on it.

You don't have to be bigger, stronger, or tougher to overcome your obstacles. You don't have to have great talent in order to do something great. When you honor God with your life, you have the most powerful force in the universe breathing in your direction. God knows how to take something ordinary and make it extraordinary.

## What You Have

*Jesus replied, "They do not need to go away. You give them something to eat." "We have here only five loaves of bread and two fish," they answered.*

MATTHEW 14:16–17

APRIL

5

Thousands of hungry people out in the middle of nowhere, and Jesus tells His disciples to give them something to eat. Impossible. But God will never ask you to do something and then not give you the ability to do it. People say, "I know I need to forgive, but it's too hard." Or "I know I should take that job, but I don't feel qualified." The truth is they have exactly what they need.

When Jesus heard the disciples' excuses, He said, "You've told me all about what you don't have. All I want to know is what you do have. Don't sit on the sidelines of life intimidated, thinking you're unqualified. Put your life, your dreams, your goals, and your talent into My hands and let Me multiply it." That's what happens when you give God what you have.

## Little into Much

*Taking the five loaves and the two fish and looking up to heaven, he gave thanks and broke the loaves. Then he gave them to the disciples, and the disciples gave them to the people. They all ate and were satisfied.*

MATTHEW 14:19–20

Compared to what you're facing now—the financial difficulty, the medical problem, or the size of your dreams—what you have may seem small. You could easily be intimidated. But God is saying, "Just give me what you have." If you'll be the best you can be right where you are, living with confidence, believing that God is breathing in your direction, then God will do for you what He did for the hungry crowd. He will take the little and turn it into much.

Still, people say, "I've got a big problem, but I don't have big resources." That's okay. God does. He owns it all. He's got you in the palm of His hand. Your obstacle may be high, but our God is the Most High. That enemy may be powerful, but God is all-powerful. He has the final say.

## Equipped and Empowered

*You will keep in perfect peace those whose minds are stead-fast, because they trust in you.*

ISAIAH 26:3

When David went to face Goliath, all he had was a slingshot and five smooth stones. It didn't look like much, and he didn't look like much, compared to the giant. But David understood this principle: Even though his slingshot was small, he realized it was given to him by God as part of his divine destiny. David ran fearlessly toward his enemy, knowing that he was equipped and empowered.

So are you overlooking something small, something ordinary, that God has given you? Are you sitting back thinking, "I don't have the talent or the education"? What is it in your life that God is breathing on and wanting to multiply? He is looking for ordinary people who will take the limits off Him, so He can show His goodness in extraordinary ways. Be confident in what you have.

*The LORD is my light and my
salvation—whom shall I fear?
The LORD is the stronghold of my
life—of whom shall I be afraid?*

PSALM 27:1

## No Excuses

When my father went to be with the Lord in 1999, I knew I was supposed to step up and pastor the church, but I had never ministered before. I thought of all the reasons I couldn't do it. I don't have the experience, the training, the booming voice, or the dynamic personality. On and on, I came up with all these excuses.

One day I heard God speak to my heart, "Joel, you've told Me all about what you don't have. I'm not interested in that. All I'm asking you to do is use what you do have." I stepped out with a little talent, a little ability, a little experience, and a little confidence. I didn't have much to give, but I realize now I had exactly what I needed. God takes the small and multiplies it.

# Anointed to Be You

*"Alas, Sovereign LORD,"*
*I said, "I do not know how*
*to speak; I am too young."*
*But the LORD said to me,*
*"Do not say, 'I am too young.'"*

APRIL

9

JEREMIAH 1:6–7

You have exactly what you need. It may seem small, but when you take the steps of faith God shows you, He'll breathe on your life and what was ordinary will become extraordinary. Now quit telling God what you don't have and what you can't do. Be confident. You may not have as much as others have, and that's okay. You're not running their race. Don't covet their talent, their looks, their personality, or their opportunities.

If God gave that to you, it wouldn't help you; it would hinder you. You're not anointed to be them; you're anointed to be you. When God breathed His life into you, He equipped you with everything you need to fulfill your destiny. You have the talent, the confidence, the strength, and the creativity to fulfill your purpose.

## Stay in Faith

*Fight the good fight of the faith.
Take hold of the eternal life to
which you were called when you
made your good confession in
the presence of many witnesses.*

1 TIMOTHY 6:12

You may feel that you have a big problem but little faith. You may be up against a major challenge in your health, your finances, or a relationship. You're up against a huge giant. Let me encourage you. It isn't necessary to have great faith. Here's how the Scripture puts it: "It's not by might, not by power, but by His Spirit." Just use the faith you have.

Sometimes, we feel like David must have felt with Goliath: "All I have is a slingshot, and he's five times my size." But you can stay in faith. You don't have to lose any sleep. Your slingshot, with God's anointing, is more powerful than a giant warrior with no anointing. We excel and go places we've never dreamed of when the Most High God breathes on our lives.

## Moving Mountains

*". . . if you have faith as small as a mustard seed,
you can say to this mountain, 'Move from here to there,'
and it will move. Nothing will be impossible for you."*

MATTHEW 17:20

When you use even small faith, God can move mountains. It is okay to say, "God, I don't know how this is going to work out. I don't know how my dreams could come to pass. I don't know how I could get over this medical situation. But God, I trust You. My life is in Your hands." Even if it's small faith, that's what allows the Creator of the universe to go to work.

Get in agreement with Him and have faith that you have exactly what you need. Don't ever say, "I don't have what it takes." Zip that up and declare, "I am anointed. I am equipped. I am empowered. I am the right size, the right nationality. I know the right people. I have the right amount of talent."

## Little Steps

*Now there were four men with leprosy at the entrance of the city gate. They said to each other, "Why stay here until we die?"*

2 KINGS 7:3

The city was surrounded by an army and starving, and four lepers realized their only hope was to go to the enemy camp. Notice they didn't have great faith. Their attitude was, "We are 99 percent sure we're going to die. What do we have to lose?" They could have stayed sitting there depressed, bitter, and blaming God. Instead, they used what they had—a little faith and a little courage.

When they arrived in the camp, nobody was there, but the army's provisions had been left behind. God had caused the enemy to hear the sound of an approaching army, and they had fled. God used the lepers' steps of faith to spare the entire city. Even just doing something small, that's when supernatural things can begin to happen. God can cause people to hear what He wants them to hear.

**How You Are Seen**

*That day the LORD exalted Joshua in the sight of all Israel; and they stood in awe of him all the days of his life, just as they had stood in awe of Moses.*

JOSHUA 4:14

Years ago I met with a salesman about a big order of television equipment for Lakewood Church. We had a good meeting. He called back in a few days and said he could give us the discount we had requested. He said it was the largest discount he had ever given in over thirty years. When I said, "That's great. What is the discount?" he responded, "What do you mean, Joel? You told me the exact price you could afford." But I hadn't given him a price at all.

Here's what I've found: God can cause others to hear what He wants them to hear. God can cause you to be seen the way He wants you to be seen. It's not how you feel that matters; it's how God causes you to be seen.

*I know the LORD is always
with me. I will not be shaken,
for he is right beside me.*

PSALM 16:8 NLT

## Stand Up Tall

You may not feel very powerful or influential, but part of faith is acting like it. Do yourself a favor. Don't tell everyone how you feel. Don't ever say, "I don't have the strength or enough money. My company could never compete." Just put your shoulders back. Stand up tall; don't act weak or intimidated, but like a child of the Most High God. Act like you're strong, anointed, confident, secure, empowered, and blessed.

You don't know how God is causing you to be seen. Because of God's favor on your life, He will cause you to be seen the way He wants you to be seen. When you stay in faith like that, God will multiply what you have. He will multiply your talent, multiply your resources, and multiply your influence.

## What's in Your Hand?

*Moses answered, "What if they do not believe me or listen to me and say, 'The LORD did not appear to you'?" Then the LORD said to him, "What is that in your hand?" "A staff," he replied.*

EXODUS 4:1–2

APRIL

# 15

When God called Moses to lead more than a million people out of Egypt, Moses asked Him how he could prove to the people that God had spoken to him. God said, "Moses, what's in your hand?" Moses looked down at his staff and said, "It's just a stick." God said, "Throw it down." He threw it down, and it turned into a snake. God said, "Pick it up." He picked it up, and it turned back into a rod.

God was showing him he had what he needed. It looked like an ordinary, insignificant rod. But if it needed to be a key to open a door, God could turn it into a key. If it needed to be a shield to protect him, God could turn it into a shield. God was saying, "I can become what you need."

## Move Forward

*But you, LORD, are a shield around me, my glory, the One who lifts my head high.*

PSALM 3:3

You may have small faith today. That's okay. Use it, and God can move mountains. You may have average talent. That's all right. Use it, and God can do something exceptional. You may feel weak, but don't you dare act weak. Put your shoulders back. Hold your head up high, and God will cause you to be seen the way He wants you to be seen.

Right now God is breathing on your dreams, your finances, your health, and your children. God is going to multiply your talent, your resources, and your creativity. This is not the time to shrink back in fear. This is the time to move forward in faith. Get up every morning knowing you are anointed. You are equipped. You are empowered. You have everything you need to fulfill your destiny.

## *Yes* Is in Your Future

*What, then, shall we say in response to these things? If God is for us, who can be against us? He who did not spare his own Son, but gave him up for us all—how will he not also, along with him, graciously give us all things?*

ROMANS 8:31–32

When God laid out the plan for your life, He had all of your *yes*es planned out—to that promotion, to a clean bill of health, to getting married, to being accepted into college. You may have been told *no* a thousand times, but God has the final say, and He says, "*Yes* is coming your way." *Yes*es are in your future.

Now here's the key: On the way to *yes* there will be *no*s. You have to go through the *no*s to get to your *yes*es. The mistake many people make is that they become discouraged by the *no*s and they quit trying. You have to go through your closed doors before you reach your open doors. When you come to a *no*, instead of being discouraged the correct attitude is: "I'm one step closer to my *yes*."

*You make known to me the path
of life; you will fill me with joy
in your presence, with eternal
pleasures at your right hand.*

PSALM 16:11

## No Is Simply a Test

What if you could see into your future and discovered you would receive twenty *no*s before you came to your *yes*? Then you'd be prepared to handle it when you faced a disappointment or a setback. You wouldn't give up if a loan didn't go through or you didn't land a big sales contract. You would just check it off and say, "All right. Now I'm only nineteen away from my *yes*." You would be encouraged every time you heard a *no*.

But too many people hit several *no*s in a row and lose their passion. You've got to get this down in your spirit. *Yes* is in your future. To be turned down, delayed, or overlooked was all a part of God's plan. The *no* is simply a test. Will you keep moving forward knowing that *yes*es are coming your way?

## Shake It Off

*"In this world you will have trouble.*
*But take heart! I have overcome the world."*

JOHN 16:33

A church member told me that his supervisor at work was about to retire, and he was in line for the job along with two coworkers. He had the most seniority and had worked for the company faithfully for many years, but he was passed over for the promotion. They chose a younger, less experienced person. He felt cheated.

The situation did not seem fair, but he understood this principle. He knew there were already *yes*es in his future put there by the Creator of the universe. He didn't grow bitter. He didn't quit being his best. He shook it off and kept working unto God. About two years later, the vice president of the company retired, and they offered him that top job. His position now is many levels higher than that supervisor position he'd been denied.

## Surrounded by Favor

*Then Jehoahaz sought the LORD's favor,*
*and the LORD listened to him, for he saw how severely*
*the king of Aram was oppressing Israel.*

2 KINGS 13:4

God knows what He is doing. You may be in a *no* right now. Maybe a relationship ended, or you were passed over for a promotion, or you lost a loved one. Don't be discouraged. Instead, say, "I may be in a *no*, but I'll never give up on my dream. I know a *yes* is coming. Favor is coming. Healing is coming. Promotion is coming. I will not become stuck in a *no*. I know *yes*es are in my future."

The Scripture says, "All of God's promises are yes and amen." We should get up every morning and say, "Father, thank you for some *yes*es today. Yes, I'm healed. Yes, I'm free. Yes, I'm surrounded by Your favor."

## Bring It to Pass

*Though I walk in the midst of trouble, You will revive me . . .*

PSALM 138:7 NKJV

I read that 90 percent of all first-time businesses fail. Ninety percent of all second-time businesses succeed. But 80 percent of those who start one business and fail never try a second time. What happened? They get stuck on a *no*. They become discouraged and think, "It didn't happen last time. It will never happen." They fail to realize they were just one *no* away from seeing it succeed.

Have you ever given up a few *no*s away from seeing a dream come to pass? What if you knew you had to go through only three more *no*s and then you would meet the right person? You would probably go out and find people to meet just to tell them *no* and get them out of the way!

*Blessed is the one who perseveres under trial because, having stood the test, that person will receive the crown of life that the Lord has promised to those who love him.*

JAMES 1:12

## One Step Closer

I have a friend who wanted to start a new business. He had tried the business concept on a small scale and succeeded. He needed his bank to loan him the money to buy some major equipment. His bank loved his business plan, but lending money was very tight. They turned him down. He could have become discouraged and given up, but he went to a second bank and was told the same thing: "It's a great idea, but . . ." Thirty-one banks said *no.*

But when God puts a dream in your heart, deep down you know that you will succeed. My friend realized that every *no* simply meant he was one step closer to his *yes.* Bank number thirty-two said, "Yes!" God had my friend's *yes,* but he had to go through thirty-one *nos* to get to it.

## Be Confident

*So do not throw away your confidence; it will be richly rewarded. You need to persevere so that when you have done the will of God, you will receive what he has promised.*

HEBREWS 10:35–36

The beautiful actress Janine Turner told me that from the time she was a little girl she dreamed of becoming an actress. As a teen, she became a model and played some small television and movie roles, but she wanted to be a more serious actress. Between the ages of fifteen and twenty-seven, she went to as many as four auditions a day and was told *no* over one thousand times. Her attitude was: "That's just another *no* out of the way. Now I'm closer to my *yes*."

And one day the top producer from a major network called her about a starring role in a new prime-time show called *Northern Exposure*. She became a star thanks to that big break, but she had to go through a thousand *no*s to get to that one *yes*.

## Keep Trying

# 24

*"Restrain your voice from weeping and your eyes from tears, for your work will be rewarded," declares the LORD.*

JEREMIAH 31:16

You may struggle with your own challenges; maybe it's a bad habit or an addiction, You think, "I have tried a thousand times to break this." I'm asking you to try one more time. You don't know when your *yes* will come. You may only be five *nos* away. Maybe the next person you meet will be your *yes*. The next college you apply to will be your *yes*.

Will you keep trying if five banks turn you down? Will you stay in faith if three medical reports in a row are not good? Will you take a chance on meeting somebody new if your last two relationships didn't work out? If you're to keep moving forward, you have to keep reminding yourself: "*Yes* is in my future. I will fulfill my destiny."

## One More Time

*Forgetting what is behind and straining toward what is ahead, I press on toward the goal to win the prize for which God has called me heavenward in Christ Jesus.*

PHILIPPIANS 3:13–14

I read about an experiment in which researchers put a barracuda and a Spanish mackerel in the same fish tank. Normally the barracuda would immediately devour the much smaller mackerel. But the researchers put an invisible glass partition between the two fish so when the barracuda went in for the kill, it slammed into the glass partition again and again. When the barracuda finally gave up, the researchers removed the glass partition. Interestingly, the barracuda never again went after the Spanish mackerel. They lived happily ever after in the same fish tank. The barracuda was conditioned by *no*s to think eating the mackerel would never happen. It didn't think there were any *yes*es in his future. If it had tried only one more time, the *yes* would have been there. Don't be like the barracuda.

*Consider it pure joy,
my brothers and sisters,
whenever you face trials of
many kinds, because you know
that the testing of your faith
produces perseverance.*

JAMES 1:2–3

## Keep Pursuing

What happened to the barracuda in yesterday's reading happens to many people after they've hit the wall many times, so to speak. You may have worked hard, but didn't get the promotion. Maybe you pursued dreams, but you ran into closed doors time and again. Like the barracuda, we've let this stronghold convince us that it will never happen.

How do you know that God has not removed the glass partition that was holding you back? How do you know that the next time you try won't be your *yes*? The partition separating you from your dream may have been up for years, but God can remove it in a split second. You'll never know unless you keep trying, you keep dreaming, you keep pursuing what God put in your heart.

## A Small *Yes*

*"Go and look toward the sea,"
he told his servant. . . . "There
is nothing there," he said. Seven
times Elijah said, "Go back." The
seventh time the servant reported,
"A cloud as small as a man's
hand is rising from the sea."*

1 KINGS 18:43–44

APRIL
27

The Prophet Elijah went to the top of Mount Carmel and prayed and asked God to end the great drought. After praying, he said to the people, "I can hear the sound of an abundance of rain." He was saying, "There's a *yes* in our future. Rain is coming." Seven times Elijah told his assistant to go and look for any sign of rain, and six times Elijah was told *no*.

After the seventh trip, the assistant came back and reported a small cloud in the sky. It wasn't much. Just the size of a man's hand. Elijah received a small *yes*, a faint *yes*, a barely-see-it *yes*, but when you're expecting things to change in your favor—when you know God has *yes* in your future—you will latch on to even a small sign by faith and soon it will pour.

128 ✦ JOEL OSTEEN

## In It to Win It

*"Stand firm,
and you will win life."*

LUKE 21:19

When Thomas Edison was trying to invent the lightbulb, he failed on his first two thousand attempts. Two thousand times he tried and it didn't work out. Two thousand times he was told *no*. He could have given up and quit, but he just kept looking for that one *yes*. After Edison came up with a working lightbulb, a reporter asked him about all of his failed experiments. He said, "I never failed once. I just found two thousand ways that wouldn't work."

Keep looking. Keep expecting. Keep dreaming. You've got to have a made-up mind. You are in it to win it. You will not let people talk you out of it. You will not give up because it didn't happen on your timetable. You will not settle for second best because a few doors have closed.

## Persistent

*We can rejoice, too, when we run into problems
and trials, for we know that they help us develop endurance.
And endurance develops strength of character . . .*

ROMANS 5:3–4 NLT

You may have had some setbacks or disappointments, or you tried something that didn't work out. These were not a waste of your time. Every challenge you've gone through has deposited something on the inside. God doesn't waste anything. You are not defined by your past. You are prepared by your past. Just because you've had some *no*s only means *yes* is still in your future. When you hit your big *yes*, all the other *no*s will become insignificant.

Do not feel badly because you're not where you want to be right this minute. Don't focus on the disappointment, the failure, or the mistakes. They were all a part of God's plan to prepare you for your *yes*. Keep moving forward, being your best, honoring God, being determined and persistent, and God promises *yes* is in your future.

## Crooked Places Straight

*"The crooked roads shall become straight, the rough ways smooth. And all people will see God's salvation."*

LUKE 3:5–6

We all face situations that seem impossible. It's easy to become discouraged and think that things will never work out. But God is going before us making our crooked places straight. You may not have the connections right now to accomplish your dreams, but you don't have to worry. God is going before you and lining up the right people. He's arranging the right breaks, the right opportunities.

You may have lost a job or had your hours cut back. It's easy to get negative and think nothing will ever change. But you have to realize this loss is not a surprise to God. He's not up in the heavens scratching His head, thinking, "Oh, no. Now what will I do?" God knew exactly when that setback would occur, and the good news is He has already arranged a solution.

**Be Your Best** | *For the Lord takes delight in his people; he crowns the humble with victory.*

PSALM 149:4

Right now, God is going before you to prepare the next chapter of your life. If you will stay in faith and keep the right attitude, you will enter a better chapter, a chapter with greater victories and greater fulfillment. Coworkers may be trying to push you down, playing politics. But when you understand this principle, you won't be upset. You won't go in there and try to play their games and prove to them who you are.

Instead, you will stay in peace, knowing that the Most High God, the Creator of the universe, the One who controls it all, is going before you. He promised to fight your battles. If you will stay on the high road and just keep being your best, you will see the hand of God at work in amazing ways.

*For this God is our God for ever and ever; he will be our guide even to the end.*

PSALM 48:14

## A Sure Guide

You may be discouraged and think that your life situation will never change. Maybe you can't see anything happening. But if the curtain was pulled back, you could see into the unseen realm. There, you would see God at work arranging things in your favor. It may not happen overnight, but at the right time, in your due season, God will not only move the wrong people out of the way, but He also will pay you back for every injustice. He will make up for lost time and guide you to where you're supposed to be.

He's planning to open this door and bring a certain person across your path. He's getting you in position for the right opportunities. He's even looking years down the road and arranging solutions to problems that you haven't had yet.

## New Days
## Are Coming

*"The days are coming," declares the LORD, "when . . . New wine will drip from the mountains and flow from all the hills . . ."*

AMOS 9:13

MAY
3

I want you to get this down in your spirit like never before: God is going before you making your crooked places straight. You may have gone through a disappointment, an unfair situation, but don't settle there. Don't sink into self-pity. In your future, God has already lined up a new beginning, new friendships, and new opportunities. It's right up ahead of you. Maybe last year was rough on your finances or in your career. If you had some setbacks, don't make the mistake of expecting this year to be the same. Get a new vision. This is a new day.

You may have taken a couple of steps backward in recent times, but let me declare over you that God will thrust you forward. God has planned explosive growth in your future.

## More Than Conquerors

*No, in all these things we are more than conquerors through him who loved us.*

ROMANS 8:37

God is going before you. That's a fact. If you have financial and career concerns, your attitude should be: "Yes, the economy is down, but I'm not worried. I know God is going before me, and He has promised He will make rivers in the desert. He will prosper me even in the midst of a recession."

If your child has strayed off course, your report should be, "I know God can do the impossible. I may not see a way, but I know God has a way. I believe God is going before my child lining up the right people to come across his path, taking away the wrong people, breaking every force of darkness, opening his eyes to every deception, and giving him the wisdom to make good choices to fulfill his destiny."

**Quickly Conquer**

*"But recognize today that the LORD your God is the one who will cross over ahead of you like a devouring fire to destroy them. He will subdue them so that you will quickly conquer . . ."*

DEUTERONOMY 9:3 NLT

The people of Israel, whom God brought out of Egypt, had settled in the wilderness, believing the enemies ahead of them were too big and their obstacles were too great. This thinking kept them from God's best. Many years later, their children and grandchildren stood by the Jordan River, about to cross over and go into the Promised Land, which was occupied by incredibly strong, powerful people called the Anakites. They were actually descendants of giants. In the natural, the people of Israel didn't have a chance. You can imagine how intimidated they must have felt knowing that they had to face these huge warriors. As they stood there at the Jordan, no doubt contemplating whether or not they should go through with it, God gave them this promise that helped push them over.

This promise is for you as well.

# MAY 6

*Hezekiah and all the people rejoiced at what God had brought about for his people, because it was done so quickly.*

2 CHRONICLES 29:36

## Be Amazed

Y ou may be facing a situation that seems as impossible as Hezekiah's. Maybe you are facing a health issue, a financial difficulty, or a legal challenge. It may appear that you don't have a chance. But God is saying to you what He said to the people of Israel: "the Lord your God is the one who will cross over ahead of you . . . He will subdue them so that you will quickly conquer . . ."

You need to receive that in your spirit. You will come out of trouble quicker than you think. You will get well quicker than you think. Your recovery will amaze the doctors. You will accomplish your dreams much quicker than you think. Supernatural breaks are coming your way. The Lord your God is crossing over ahead of you.

## You Can

*At that time Joshua went and destroyed the
Anakites from the hill country . . .*

JOSHUA 11:21

The Scripture says: "Who can stand up to the
Anakites? They're descendants of giants." In
modern-day terms your concerns would be more
like: "The economy is down. You can't be blessed.
You can't be successful this year." Or, "The medical report says you're very sick and might never
be healthy again." Or, "Your coach said you're not
talented. You don't have what it takes."

The next time something is discouraging
to you, just give the same reply God gave to the
people of Israel. "Yes, it may look impossible. All
the odds are against me. I'm not denying the
facts. But I'm not worried about them. I know
God has the final say, and He has promised He
will cross over ahead of me and defeat my challenges for me. So my declaration is, 'I will quickly
conquer them.'"

## None Like Him

*"Lord, the God of Israel, there is no God like you in heaven above or on earth below—you who keep your covenant of love with your servants who continue wholeheartedly in your way."*

1 KINGS 8:23

The obstacles trying to hold you back don't have a chance when you switch over into faith. Get in agreement with God. Nothing can stand against our God. Turn around those negative thoughts that say you will never get well, never accomplish your dreams, or never overcome an addiction. Make a declaration of faith instead: "I will overcome this addiction quickly." "I will get well quickly." "I will accomplish my dreams much quicker than I think."

You won't do this by your own strength or by your own power. You will accomplish this because Almighty God, the One who holds your future in His hands, will go before you, fighting your battles, and making crooked places straight.

## No Coincidences

*"I make known the end from the beginning, from ancient times, what is still to come. I say, 'My purpose will stand, and I will do all that I please.'"*

ISAIAH 46:10

Several years ago, I became friends with a man who installed equipment in our church office. However, he lived in another state, so I saw him only once or twice over the next few years. Then, twelve years later, Victoria and I came into a once-in-a-lifetime business opportunity in his field of expertise. The first thing I did was call him, and over a period of time he negotiated a very complicated contract and put it all together. The business became a huge success.

I realize now God brought him into our lives not just for the friendship, but for that specific purpose, too. You may think that you met someone just by accident. But one day you will look back and see how God used that person to help you move closer to your divine destiny.

*"Have you not heard?*
*Long ago I ordained it. In*
*days of old I planned it; now*
*I have brought it to pass . . ."*

ISAIAH 37:26

## His Plans

My brother, Paul, and a group of surgeons were in Haiti operating on many of the injured people from the big earthquake when the main monitor they'd been using to check patients' vital signs stopped working. Without that monitor it was too dangerous to continue the surgeries. At first they had no success in locating a replacement, but then they prayed. Not long afterward, the administrator of the hospital, a Haitian man, walked in carrying a brand-new monitor still in the box, never used. Two years previous he had attended a convention for hospital administrators in America and won this monitor as a door prize.

Two years before the problem occurred— two years before the big earthquake—God had already provided a solution. No problem is too great.

## Be Strong

*"Be strong and courageous. Do not be afraid; do not be discouraged, for the LORD your God will be with you wherever you go."*

JOSHUA 1:9

MAY
# 11

Right now, God is crossing over ahead of you. He is lining up the right people, the right supplies, and the right circumstances. He knows what you will need a week from now, a month from now, even ten years from now. And the good news is, He's already taken care of it. Quit worrying about how it will work out. God is saying to you what He said to Joshua, "Be strong and of good courage." You have someone fighting for you. The Creator of the universe is breathing in your direction. His hand of favor is upon your life. He is crossing over ahead of you, making your crooked places straight. As long as you live a life to honor Him, God has promised nothing will be able to stand up against you.

## God Knows

*The LORD will keep you from all harm—he will watch over your life; the LORD will watch over your coming and going both now and forevermore.*

PSALM 121:7–8

Remember how Captain Chesley "Sully" Sullenberger safely landed his disabled airplane on the Hudson River in New York with 150 or so people on board in January 2009? The plane had no power. The situation looked impossible. But Captain Sullenberger is an incredibly experienced pilot and is considered one of the leading experts in flight safety in the world. Not only that, Captain Sully is a certified glider pilot. For thirty-six years he has been flying planes with no power. Amazingly, the one flight that would lose power in all the engines would be piloted by the one man you would choose to be at those controls if you had planned it ten years in advance.

God knows what He is doing. He can see the big picture. God knows what's in your future: every setback, every disappointment, and every danger.

## Through Every Challenge

*Be on your guard;*
*stand firm in the faith;*
*be courageous; be strong.*

1 CORINTHIANS 16:13

Perhaps as you read yesterday's devotional, you asked, "So if God is in control, why didn't He stop the birds from hitting the engines of Captain Sullenberger's plane in the first place?" God will not stop every adversity or prevent every challenge. But if we will stay in faith, God promises He will bring us through every challenge and get us wherever we're supposed to be. I like the saying, "God never promised us smooth sailing, but He did promise us a safe landing."

Sometimes God will allow challenges just to display His goodness in a greater way. Do you know that news reports all over the world led their newscasts with stories about the "Miracle on the Hudson." People who did not believe in God were scratching their heads and saying, "That had to be divine intervention."

*The steps of a good man are
ordered by the L ORD: and he
delighteth in his way. Though he
fall, he shall not be utterly cast
down: for the L ORD upholdeth
him with his hand.*

PSALM 37:23–24 KJV

## The Advantage

I want you to have a new confidence, knowing that as a believer you have an advantage. The Creator of the universe is not only fighting your battles, He also is lining up the right people, the right breaks, and the right opportunities. Just as with Joshua, God is crossing over ahead of you. Just as with Captain Sully, God will place the right people in your path. Just as with my brother, Paul, and the surgery monitor, God has the solution before you had the problem.

You may be facing a situation that looks like it will never turn around. Let me declare this over you: You will see it turn around quicker than you think. You will come out of debt quicker than you think. You will accomplish your destiny much quicker than you think.

## The Gracious Hand of God

*"The gracious hand of our God is on everyone who looks to him . . ."*

EZRA 8:22

MAY

# 15

If you've seen the television show *The X Factor*, you know the judges are looking for contestants who have that indefinable something that makes them stand out as performers. No one can define exactly what that special quality is. It's not just talent, not just looks, not just personality. There's just something about them that makes them special, something that gives them an advantage. They call it the X Factor.

When God breathed His life into you, He put something in you to give you an advantage. There is something about you that makes you stand out, something that draws opportunity, something that causes you to overcome obstacles, to accomplish dreams. On that television show they call it the X Factor, but the Scripture calls it "the gracious hand of God."

## The Favor Factor

*. . . nor did their own arm save them; but it was Your right hand, Your arm, and the light of Your countenance, because You favored them.*

PSALM 44:3 NKJV

God's favor is something special. You can't put your finger on it. But you know this is not just your talent, your education, or your hard work. It's not just good fortune, not just a lucky break. It's Almighty God breathing in your direction. It's the gracious hand of God giving His blessing on your life. You could call it "the favor factor."

As Psalm 44 says, the victories you've seen in the past weren't just your own doing. God favored you. You wouldn't be where you are if the gracious hand of God was not on your life. Every accomplishment, every good break, every obstacle you've overcome, was God opening the door, God bringing the right people, God turning it around. The Creator of the universe was smiling down on you. His gracious hand is at work in your life.

## You Have It

*When his master saw that the LORD was with him*
*and that the LORD gave him success in everything he did,*
*Joseph found favor in his eyes and became his attendant.*

GENESIS 39:3–4

You may not have as much education as somebody else or come from the most influential family. But that's okay. You have an advantage. Deep down you know there is something about you that is indefinable. Other people won't be able to figure it out. All they know is you've got it—something they like, something that causes you to succeed. God's favor can take you where you cannot go on your own.

When you realize you have this advantage, an edge, you'll go out each day not intimidated by your dreams, not discouraged or thinking that the problem is too big. No, you'll put your shoulders back. You'll hold your head up high and go out with a spring in your step, confident, secure, knowing that you have what it takes. You have the favor of God.

## "Yes, I Can"

*And the LORD was with him; he was successful
in whatever he undertook.*

### 2 KINGS 18:7

Recently a friend told me that he wanted to start a business, had done all this great research, and put together a fantastic presentation. But then he realized he didn't have enough experience in this type of business. On paper, he wasn't qualified. His heart told him, "Yes, I can do this," but his mind kept coming up with reasons why it would not work out.

Remind yourself that because you keep God in first place, there is something about you that can't be put on paper, something that's indefinable. It's Almighty God breathing in your direction. It's God causing good breaks to come. It's the right people being attracted to you. It's the Still Small Voice giving you inside information, letting you know things that are critical to your success and can't be measured.

**More and More**

*And he became more and more powerful, because the LORD God Almighty was with him.*

2 SAMUEL 5:10

One of our Lakewood members had a small computer company with only three employees, yet a new client came to him from a competitor that was more than a hundred times his size, with offices all over the world and practically unlimited resources. But this client said, "We like your work. We're going to move our account to your firm." Now his company is outperforming a competitor many, many times his size. That other company's executives are scratching their heads, thinking, "What is it with this man?" It's God's favor causing him to stand out and causing people to be drawn to him.

You may not have all the talent, training, and experience, but because you honor God, His favor can cause you to go farther than people who should be running circles around you.

*Solomon son of David
established himself firmly over
his kingdom, for the LORD his
God was with him and made
him exceedingly great.*

2 CHRONICLES 1:1

## Quiet Confidence

It's not how influential or educated someone is; when you have the favor factor, you have an advantage. God's favor opens the right doors and brings good breaks. The favor of God will cause you to accomplish what you could not accomplish on your own. It gives you an edge.

Now, if you're to see the gracious hand of God at work, you can't go through the day intimidated. You have to carry yourself as if you have God's hand on you. You have to think like you have favor, talk like you have favor, walk like you have favor, and dress like you have favor. Not arrogantly, thinking that you're better than somebody else, but just living with this quiet confidence, knowing that you have an advantage. You have an edge. The gracious hand of God is on your life.

## Everything Needed

*And because the gracious hand of my God was on me, the king granted my requests.*

NEHEMIAH 2:8

MAY
# 21

When Nehemiah heard that the walls of Jerusalem had been torn down, God put a dream in his heart to rebuild those walls. In the natural it was impossible. He was living more than a thousand miles away, working as a cupbearer to the Persian king. He didn't have the money, the manpower, or the influence. But Nehemiah had the favor factor.

When he asked the king for permission to go back to Jerusalem and build those walls, the king not only said yes but he gave Nehemiah letters of protection and the materials he needed to complete the task. Even though he had no experience or the resources and faced untold opposition, the favor of God helped him to overcome them. It should have taken them at least a year to complete the walls, but they did it in just fifty-two days.

## Brag on God's Favor

*I also told them about the
gracious hand of my God
on me and what the king had
said to me. They replied,
"Let us start rebuilding."*

NEHEMIAH 2:18

When you understand you have the same favor as Nehemiah had, you'll rise up with confidence and pursue what God has placed in your heart. Nehemiah arrived in Jerusalem and saw the city was in total disarray, much worse than he expected. He found some people and shared how the gracious hand of God was on his life to rebuild the walls. Notice how Nehemiah was always bragging on God's favor. No doubt some of them said, "Nehemiah, you're not a builder and don't have the experience. This is impossible."

But Nehemiah's boldness based on the gracious hand of God overcame the doubters. They started rebuilding the walls despite all kinds of opposition and attempts to shut them down. Nehemiah faced one challenge after another, but the favor of God helped him to overcome them.

## More of His Favor

*Because the hand of the LORD my God was on me, I took courage and gathered leaders from Israel to go up with me.*

EZRA 7:28

When you realize God's hand of favor is upon you, you will accomplish your dreams faster than you ever thought possible. You may be facing a situation like Nehemiah that seems impossible. Don't go around talking about how big the problem is, or how you're never going to make it, whether it's your finances, health, addictions, or dreams. Zip that up and do as Nehemiah did. Declare: "The gracious hand of God is upon my life." The more you brag on God's favor, the more of His favor you will see.

We wouldn't be considering Nehemiah today if he had thought, "I'm just average. I'd love to rebuild the walls, but I don't have the money. My boss will never let me off. I live too far away." Don't disqualify yourself. God's gracious hand is on you.

*By this I know that You favor and delight in me, because my enemy does not triumph over me.*

PSALM 41:11 AMP

## More Than Ever

Quit telling yourself the dream is too great or the obstacles are too high. It will not happen in your own strength. It will not happen in your own power. It will happen because Almighty God favors you. The victory will come because God smiles down on you. Get in agreement with God. Don't go around thinking negative, self-defeating thoughts. Instead, say: "Father, thank You that Your gracious hand is upon me. I know I have an advantage. I have an edge. Other people may not see it. They may try to push me down and disqualify me. But that's okay. I know the truth. I have the favor factor. I'm well able to fulfill my destiny."

When you are in difficult times, you need to declare God's favor over your life more than ever.

## Believe First

*You have granted me life and favor,*
*and Your providence has preserved my spirit.*

JOB 10:12 AMP

Job went through a period in which everything that could go wrong did. He lost his children, his business, his health, and his wife told him to just curse God and die. He had plenty of opportunities to be negative, bitter, and to blame God. In the natural it didn't look like Job had any favor. Instead, Job understood this principle: In the midst of the adversity, he declared that the favor of God would keep his enemies from defeating him. No wonder Job eventually came out restored and healed with twice what he had before.

This is what faith is all about. You can't wait until you see it before you decide to believe it. You have to believe it first and then you'll see it. Your attitude will determine the outcome.

## Speak Favor

*"But he knows the way that I take; when
he has tested me, I will come forth as gold."*

JOB 23:10

What causes God to defeat our enemies, what causes Him to give us breakthroughs and supernatural abilities, is our offering of thanks to God for His favor, even though we don't see any sign of favor. He steps in when you say, "Father, thank You that Your gracious hand is upon me," even though nothing is going your way. Or when you say, "Lord, I know I've got what it takes," even though you feel unqualified, inferior.

That's what allows God to do amazing things. Job would have remained defeated if he had just sat back and thought, "Well, I'm a good person. I love the Lord. I hope God will do something about this trouble." Instead, Job came out with the victory because he kicked his faith into gear and spoke favor in the midst of the adversity.

### Release Power

> *For the LORD God is a sun and shield; the LORD bestows favor and honor; no good thing does he withhold from those whose walk is blameless.*

PSALM 84:11

There is a small fish called a Moses sole found in the Red Sea that typically would be eaten by large sharks. But scientists discovered that whenever the Moses sole senses any kind of danger, it secretes poisonous toxins from its glands. The toxins literally cause the sharks' jaws to freeze.

That's what the Scripture means when it says, "The favor of God will keep my enemies from defeating me." Every time you say, "Lord, thank You that Your gracious hand is upon me," toxins are released that paralyze the enemy. But just the opposite happens if you go around talking about how big your problems are. If you are negative, worried, or start complaining, you attract more difficulty. But if you'll dare to just declare God's favor, it will release a power to paralyze your enemies.

*Now God had caused the official to show favor and compassion to Daniel . . .*

DANIEL 1:9

## Crowned with Favor

When you really understand that you have God's favor, you won't become bent out of shape when trouble comes your way. Think about the little Moses sole we considered yesterday. When it's in the shark's mouth, the little fish doesn't become depressed and say, "Oh, this is not my day."

Instead, he goes about his business. He knows there is something special about him. Before the foundation of the world God ordained that he would be protected from that enemy, so he just rests in who God made him to be. When you have a revelation that you are a child of the Most High God, crowned with favor, then when adversity comes, you won't get worried or all bent out of shape. Like this little fish, you'll declare God's favor and you'll know that those enemies cannot keep you defeated.

## Do Your Part

*May the favor of the Lord our God rest on us; establish the work of our hands for us— yes, establish the work of our hands.*

PSALM 90:17

MAY

# 29

You have God's favor factor. It can't be measured. There is something about you that can't be put on paper. The bottom line is, you've got what it takes. Now do your part and activate this favor. In the tough times, don't complain. Be like Job and say, "Lord, thank You. I know I have Your favor."

When the dream looks too big, don't give up. Be like Nehemiah and all through the day pray, "Lord, thank You that Your gracious hand is upon me." If you'll do that, then like Job you will overcome every obstacle. Like Nehemiah, you will accomplish every God-given dream. I believe and declare you will become everything God has created you to be, and you will have everything God intended for you to have.

## God-Sized Prayers

*The effective, fervent prayer of a
righteous man avails much.*

JAMES 5:16 NKJV

How you pray determines what kind of life you live. If you only pray small, ordinary, get-by prayers, you'll live a small, ordinary, get-by life. But when you have the boldness to ask God for big things, you ask Him to open doors that might otherwise never open. You ask Him to take you further than anyone in your family. You ask Him to restore a relationship that looks over and done.

When you pray God-sized prayers, you will see the greatness of God's power. All through the Scripture we see this principle. Elijah prayed that it wouldn't rain, and for three and a half years there was no rain. Joshua prayed for more daylight, and God stopped the sun. Elisha prayed for protection, and his enemies standing right in front of him didn't recognize him. God made him invisible.

## Dare to Ask

*"Ask and it will be given to you; seek and you will find; knock and the door will be opened to you. For everyone who asks receives; the one who seeks finds; and to the one who knocks, the door will be opened."*

MATTHEW 7:7–8

If you're to reach your highest potential, you have to have the boldness to ask God to do the unthinkable. When was the last time you asked God to do something impossible, or something out of the ordinary? One reason we don't see God do great things is that we ask only for small things. There should be something you're praying about and asking for that seems impossible, far out, something that you cannot achieve on your own.

The phrase I hear in my spirit is *Dare to ask.* Your dream may seem impossible. You may feel you don't have the connections or the funding, but God is saying, "Dare to ask Me to bring it to pass. Dare to ask Me to connect you to the right people. Dare to ask Me to pour out a flood of My favor."

*"And I will do whatever you ask in my name, so that the Father may be glorified in the Son. You may ask me for anything in my name, and I will do it."*

JOHN 14:13–14

## Elevate Your Prayers

A lot of times we pray for small things. God meets us at the level of our faith. If you ask small, you'll receive small. Elevate your prayers.

A God-sized prayer is: "God, I'm asking You to not only turn my child around but use him in a great way." A God-sized prayer is: "God, I'm asking you to increase me in such a way that I can not only pay off my house but I can also pay off someone else's home." A God-sized prayer is: "God, help me to take our family to a new level. Let me set a new standard. When people look back two hundred years from now, let them say it was that man, or that woman, who thrust our family higher than we have ever been before."

## Simply Ask

*You do not have because you do not ask God.*

JAMES 4:2

# JUNE
# 2

I wonder how many of your prayers are not being answered simply because you're not asking. You may tell yourself: "If God wants to bless me, He'll bless me." But if you're not asking, you're not receiving, and if you're not asking big, you're shortchanging yourself. You will never reach your highest potential if you pray only small prayers.

I'm not suggesting that you can make a wish list and pray for every whim. I'm encouraging you to ask God for what He's promised you. There are dreams and desires the Creator of the universe has placed in your heart. You can tell a desire or dream is from God if it involves something bigger or grander than you could ever accomplish or acquire on your own. They're a part of your divine destiny.

## Nothing Too Hard

*"Ah, Sovereign LORD, you have made the heavens and the earth by your great power and outstretched arm. Nothing is too hard for you."*

JEREMIAH 32:17

Faith is what pleases God. Faith is what allows Him to do the impossIble. God will put something so big where you realize you don't have all the talent, the connections, or the confidence. He'll allow an obstacle to come across your path, one that you cannot overcome under your own strength.

When this happens, you can talk yourself out of your dreams and desires. Or you can say, "God, I can't do this on my own, but I know You are all-powerful. You have no limitations. There is nothing too difficult for You, so God, I'm asking for Your favor to shine down on me. I'm asking You to make a way, even though I don't see a way. God, I'm asking You to open doors that no man can shut."

## Because God Promised

*"You, my God, have revealed to your servant that you will build a house for him. So your servant has found courage to pray to you."*

1 CHRONICLES 17:25

You need boldness to ask big. In 1 Chronicles 17, God promised David that one of his descendants would always be on the throne. David could have said, "God, I'm just a small shepherd boy." Instead, David understood this promise and dared to pray, "God, I'm asking You for something big, not because I have all the talent, education, and connections, but simply because You promised it."

The dreams God has placed in your heart may seem impossible. But you have to say, "God, You promised it, now I'm bold enough to ask You for it." When you do, don't be surprised if you have doubts. The enemy gets stirred up when you start asking God for big things. Negative thoughts will come: "Who do you think you are?" Just smile and reply, "I am a child of the Most High God."

## Anything

*"I am the LORD, the God of all mankind.
Is anything too hard for me?"*

JEREMIAH 32:27

A minister I know had a four-year-old son who found his goldfish floating on the top of the water, totally stiff. The little boy asked with great sadness, "Dad, can we ask God to heal my fish?" The minister wanted his son to know that he could pray about anything. But he also wanted to make it clear that sometimes our prayers aren't answered in the way we want. Finally he said, "Yes, son, let's pray."

Early the next morning, the father heard his son shout, "Yes!" The goldfish was swimming around as healthy as can be. That dad nearly passed out. Before seeing the fish come alive, the father had his speech prepared, which he abandoned and said, "God, You can do anything." God encourages us to just believe and stay in faith. That's what allows Him to do the extraordinary.

### The Father's Pleasure

*"Do not be afraid, little flock, for your Father has been pleased to give you the kingdom."*

LUKE 12:32

Have you talked yourself out of dreams? Have you convinced yourself that you will never overcome certain challenges? Why don't you take the limits off God? What if your dreams aren't happening because you're not being bold enough to ask? God wants to give you the desires of your heart, but you have to have the faith of a child and be willing to ask.

As a father, I would rather bless my own children than anyone else. Who would any father most enjoy seeing excel and fulfill their dreams? Nobody more than his own children. That's the way it is with our Heavenly Father, too. It is His pleasure to give you the Kingdom. That brings a smile to His face. But you must step up and ask Him.

*Ask me, and I will make the nations your inheritance, the ends of the earth your possession.*

PSALM 2:8

## Ask Big

Quit asking small. Quit acting like you're bothering God. Quit praying weak, get-by prayers. Your Father owns it all. He created the universe. If you want to see the fullness of what He has in store, you should learn to ask big. There are things I pray in privacy that I've never told another person. These are my secret petitions. If I shared them, you'd think: "Are you serious? You really think that could happen?"

The fact is they may not all come to pass, but if I don't reach my highest potential, it shouldn't be because I failed to ask God's help. I don't want to get to Heaven and have God say: "Joel, I had all this for you—abundance, good breaks, wisdom, favor, healing, and restoration—but you never asked. I wanted you to pray God-sized prayers."

# It Will Be Done

*"If you remain in me and my words remain in you, ask whatever you wish, and it will be done for you."*

JOHN 15:7

JUNE

# 8

I believe one reason I've seen God's favor in my life is that I've learned to ask big. When my father died and I had never ministered before, I prayed a bold prayer asking God to help me not only to maintain what my parents have built, but also for God to let me go further. It was a bold prayer when I met Victoria for the first time and prayed: "God, please let her see how good-looking I am!" It was a bold prayer to ask God to help us build our church in the arena where the Rockets used to play basketball.

I look back and wonder what would not have happened if I had not prayed bold prayers. It's good to ask God for your needs, but I'm challenging you to ask for your dreams.

## He Hears Our Cry

*He fulfills the desires of those who fear him; he hears their cry and saves them.*

**PSALM 145:19**

Back in the 1960s, by the time Victor Torres was fourteen he was in a gang, hooked on heroin, and had already been involved in stealing, robbing, and mugging. His heartbroken mother didn't just pray that God would protect him and set him free from the drugs. She asked God to make him a minister and use him to bring other young men to God. She would hug him and speak faith into her son. One day, Victor came across David Wilkerson preaching on a New York City street corner. Victor responded to Wilkerson's message and his life was transformed. In that moment, God touched his life. Today, Victor Torres is not only free from drugs; he is the pastor of a great church, New Life Outreach in Richmond, Virginia, and holds huge outreaches to drug addicts and gang members.

## Keep Asking

*"But as for me and my household, we will serve the LORD."*

JOSHUA 24:15

Perhaps you have a family member who has made poor choices and you're just about to write them off. It may seem like this relative will never get better. I encourage you to keep on asking God to not only bring this person back, but also to help your relative do something great. I've found when God touches somebody who has been living a radically wrong kind of life, the person begins living a radically right kind of life.

It says in Psalms that the seed of the righteous will be mighty in the land—exceptional, powerful, amazing. Pray a bold prayer over your children: "God, I'm asking that my children will be mighty in the land. I'm asking You to use them in amazing ways. Let them leave a legacy of faith that will be seen for generations to come."

*"Test me in this," says the LORD Almighty, "and see if I will not throw open the floodgates of heaven and pour out so much blessing that there will not be room enough to store it."*

MALACHI 3:10

## Floods of Favor

During a recent Lakewood service, I prayed with a college student who had just completed her master's degree program in medical research. I don't even know why I said it, but I prayed, "God, let her find the cure for cancer. Let her make an astounding difference." She started weeping and said, "That's what my parents have prayed over me ever since I was a little child." Someone might ask: "What if it doesn't happen?" I prefer to think, "What if it does?"

God is saying, "Ask Me to open the floodgates of Heaven and pour out floods of favor, floods of mercy, and floods of My goodness. I dare you to ask. I dare you to take the limits off Me. I dare you to think bigger. I dare you to stretch your faith. I dare you to pray God-sized prayers."

## What Do You Want?

*Jesus stopped and called them.*
*"What do you want me to do for you?"*

MATTHEW 20:32

In Matthew 20, Jesus approached two blind men who were shouting, "Jesus, please have mercy on us!" He asked them something interesting: "What do you want Me to do for you?" It was obvious what they wanted. Why would Jesus ask what they wanted? He wanted to know what they believed. They could have said, "It's hard because we're blind. We just need somebody to take care of us. We need shelter."

These two men did not disappoint Jesus. They were bold. They said, "Lord, we want our eyes to be open." When Jesus heard their request, He touched their eyes and for the first time they could see. Imagine Jesus standing before you right now, and He is asking you: "What is it you want Me to do?" Your answer will determine what God does.

## Break Strongholds

*The weapons we fight with are not the weapons of the world. On the contrary, they have divine power to demolish strongholds.*

### 2 CORINTHIANS 10:4

I want to remind you of what God said in the Psalms: "Open your mouth wide, and I will fill it." My question is: How wide open is your mouth? What are you asking for? Are you praying bold prayers? It's not enough to just think it. It's not enough to just hope something supernatural happens. When you ask, God releases favor, strongholds are broken, and the Most High God begins to breathe in your direction.

God has put seeds of greatness on the inside. He wants you to leave your mark on our generation. You're not supposed to come and go and nobody miss you. Break out of your box. Ask God for the secret petitions He's placed on the inside. If you can accomplish it on your own, it's not a God-sized dream. Enlarge your vision.

### You Will Receive

*"Ask and you will receive, and your joy will be complete."*

JOHN 16:24

It was after two o'clock in the morning, and we were stuck at the airport because my mother's car battery was dead. We tried jumper cables, but the engine wouldn't turn over. A mechanic came, but he couldn't make it happen. My brother, Paul, told my mother, "It won't start; just ride with me and we'll get the car tomorrow," but she needed it in the morning and refused to leave. We tried again, without success. Finally she said, "Give me the keys." She got in that car and started praying out loud. All of the sudden, we heard the car crank right up. She revved that engine like she was running a race at Daytona and just left us there standing in her dust.

When you face situations that seem impossible, God says, "I dare you to pray."

> *He will call on me, and I will answer him; I will be with him in trouble, I will deliver him and honor him.*
>
> PSALM 91:15

# Call on Him

You may think God has bigger things to deal with than getting a car started. But you are God's biggest deal. You are the apple of His eye. So often we limit God. We have a small view of Him. We think He's over there busy running the universe. "I can't bother God with these small things. I can only pray if I'm facing a major catastrophe."

God knows the number of hairs on your head. He knows your thoughts before you think them and your words before you speak them. You're not inconveniencing God by asking for help in your everyday life. God wants to be good to you. He wants to show you His favor in new ways. He's saying today, "I dare you to ask Me to start your car."

## Great and Unsearchable

*"Call to me and I will answer you and tell you great and unsearchable things you do not know."*

JEREMIAH 33:3

JUNE

# 16

A small church in the foothills of the Smoky Mountains built a new sanctuary on donated land only to be informed by the building inspector that unless they doubled the parking spaces they could not open. The problem was they had used every part of their property except the huge hill behind them. Church members showed up at a special prayer meeting and after an hour of prayer, the pastor announced, "God has never let us down before. We will open as scheduled."

The next morning a construction foreman showed up at the church and said, "Reverend, we're building a shopping center nearby and need fill dirt. If you'll sell us that huge hill of dirt, we'll also pave all the areas where we dig up." They got their parking lot for free and moved into their new building as scheduled!

## God Will Show Up

*The eyes of the LORD are on the righteous, and his ears are attentive to their cry . . . he delivers them from all their troubles.*

PSALM 34:15, 17

When you pray God-sized prayers, God will show up in a big way. You may not be seeing great things, because you're asking only for small things. God Is saying, "Ask Me to open doors that look impossible. Ask Me to connect you to the right people. Ask Me for that business you've dreamed about."

If you're to become everything God's created you to be, you need a boldness to ask big. Like David, you must say, "God, You promised it. I see it here in the Scripture. Now I will be bold enough to ask You for it." If you'll learn to pray these God-sized prayers, you'll see your children become mighty in the land, the right people will show up at the right time, and God will give you the desires of your heart.

## Remind God

*. . . you who [are His servants and by your prayers] put the Lord in remembrance [of His promises], keep not silence . . .*

ISAIAH 62:6 AMP

One of the most powerful ways to pray is to find a promise in the Scripture and remind God what He said about you. "God, You said I'm blessed and cannot be cursed . . . with long life You would satisfy me . . . Your favor is not for a season but for a lifetime." When you can say, "God, You said . . . ," all of Heaven comes to attention. God is faithful to His Word.

It says to put God in remembrance of His promises, not your problems. Prayer is not an excuse to complain or a self-pity session. All that will do is make you more discouraged. If you want to see things change, if you want God to turn it around, instead of complaining find a promise you can stand on.

*So Abraham called that place
The Lord Will Provide.*

**GENESIS 22:14**

# Jehovah Jireh

When you put God in remembrance of His promises, you allow God to bring them to pass. You may not feel well. The medical report is not good. You could easily say, "God, I don't see how I will ever get well." Rather than put God in remembrance of your problems, put God in remembrance of His promises. "God, You said You would restore health unto me and heal me of my wounds. You said I would live and not die. You said what is impossible with men is possible with God."

Remind God that He has said He will supply all of your needs according to His riches. He said He is Jehovah Jireh; the Lord our provider. He said He would fight our battles. He said what is meant for our harm He will use to our advantage.

## "God, You Said . . ."

*Remember your word*
*to your servant, for you*
*have given me hope.*

PSALM 119:49

# JUNE
# 20

When you pray God's promises instead of praying the problems, you will feel better, and it will change your attitude from a victim's to a victor's. God's Word coming out of your mouth is alive and powerful.

When God hears His promises, He dispatches angels with the answers. He sets the miracle into motion. He will change things in your favor. It may not happen overnight, but just stay in faith and keep reminding God what He promised you day in and day out. Instead of begging, remind Him: "God, You said . . ." Instead of describing the circumstances, bring up His promises: "God, You said . . ." If you will get in a habit of saying, "God, You said . . . ," eventually you will see what God said come to pass in your life.

## God Cannot Lie

JUNE

# 21

*. . . in the hope of eternal life, which God, who does not lie, promised before the beginning of time . . .*

TITUS 1:2

O ur daughter, Alexandra, has been hooked on going to Disneyland since she was three years old. Now she is a teenager, and one night she said, "Daddy, I want to go back to Disneyland. Will you take me?" I didn't think much about it. I just said in passing, "Sure. I'll take you sometime." "You promise?" "Yes, I promise." I didn't know she was going to remind me of my promise a thousand times. It wasn't long before we were back at Disneyland.

When we promise our children something, we will do everything possible to bring that promise to pass. If we as earthly parents are that moved when our children remind us of what we've promised—to respond to the *you saids*—how much more will our Heavenly Father stand behind His Word? He cannot lie.

## The Promises God Made

*"Now, LORD, the God of Israel, keep for your servant David my father the promises you made to him when you said, 'You shall never fail to have a successor to sit before me on the throne of Israel . . .'"*

### 2 CHRONICLES 6:16

As parents, we can break promises to our children, but God cannot go against His Word. All of His promises are yes and amen.

You need to find some *You said*s. "Father, You said I will lend and not borrow." Remind God of that again and again. Maybe business is slow, and you don't see how your situation could work out. Don't go to God with that. Take a *You said*. "Father, You said You would open the windows of Heaven." "You said my cup would run over." "You said whatever I touch will succeed." "You said You would prosper me even in a desert."

When you're constantly reminding God of what He said, you are releasing your faith.

## Turn It Around

*"Praise be to the LORD, who has given rest to his people Israel just as he promised. Not one word has failed of all the good promises he gave through his servant Moses."*

### 1 KINGS 8:56

I talked to a lady whose seventeen-year marriage was coming to an end. She was devastated. Her husband had left her for someone else. Her whole world looked like it was falling apart. In that situation, it's easy to get depressed and fall into self-pity and not have any hope for the future. But I told her what I am telling you: You've got to find some *You said*s. "Father, You said You would give me beauty for ashes." "God, You said You would pay me back double for the unfair things that have happened." "God, You said all things are going to work together for my good."

When you're tempted to fall into self-pity, just turn it around and declare a *You said*. All through the day we should be putting God in remembrance of His promises.

### Does He Not Fulfill?

*"God is not human, that he should lie, not a human being, that he should change his mind. Does he speak and then not act? Does he promise and not fulfill?"*

NUMBERS 23:19

Isaiah 62:6–7 says, "Put the Lord in remembrance [of His promises], keep not silence, and give Him no rest . . ." When you are standing on a promise, you can't remind God one time and think that's good enough. "Keep not silence." That means you have to be persistent. You've got to show God you mean business. Not nagging God, not begging God, but in faith going to God relentlessly and reminding Him over and over what He promised you.

All throughout the day, and especially when the doubts arise, kick it into gear. "Father, You said the moment I pray the tide of the battle turns." "God, You said I am more than a conqueror." "God, You said You hold victory in store for the upright." It's not enough to do it one time and think you're done.

*". . . if you keep knocking long enough, he will get up and give you whatever you need because of your shameless persistence."*

LUKE 11:8 NLT

## Shameless Persistence

In Luke 18:1–8, Jesus told a parable about an unfair, unjust judge who had been unwilling to listen to a widow's case. However, she knew the law was on her side. She kept going back day after day, week after week, and finally he ruled in her favor because of her "continual coming" or "constant requests." That's the way we need to be when it comes to reminding God what He said.

The good news is, God is not like this judge. God is for us. But if we're to see His promises come to pass, we must have this shameless persistence. Some promises you may have to stand on for a year, or five years, or twenty years. Whatever the case, you should have a made-up mind. You are not remaining silent. You know what belongs to you.

## God Is Faithful

*"Present your case," says the*
*LORD. "Set forth your argu-*
*ments," says Jacob's King.*

ISAIAH 41:21

JUNE

# 26

My sister Lisa and her husband, Kevin, had been trying to have a baby for six years. So she listed on a piece of paper all of the promises she was standing on concerning having a baby. She made it like a legal contract: "God, You said in Genesis 1:28 to be fruitful and multiply. You said in Psalm 112 our children would be mighty in the land. You said in Psalm 113 that You make the barren woman a happy mother of children. Now we're presenting our case based on Your Word, knowing that You are faithful and true to what You have said."

Week after week, she just kept reminding God what He had promised. About two years later, God blessed them with twins, and today they have three beautiful children. God is faithful to His Word.

## Jesus, Our Advocate

*. . . we have an advocate with the Father—Jesus Christ, the Righteous One.*

1 JOHN 2:1

My questions are: Are you presenting your case to God? Have you found the promise He made so you can say, "God, You said . . ."? Have you set forth your argument? If you present your case before God, the good news is that Jesus is our "advocate" or "lawyer." In the courtroom of Heaven, imagine Jesus is our lawyer. God is the judge. Jesus will be faithful and true to His Word.

Make a list of the promises you're standing on. Put it up somewhere where you will see it often. All through the day, week after week, especially when those thoughts come telling you that His promise will not come to pass, just keep reminding God what He promised you. As long as you present your case based on God's Word, you cannot lose.

### State Your Case

*"Put Me in remembrance; let us contend together; state your case . . ."*

ISAIAH 43:26 NKJV

Sometimes, especially when we're in real difficulty, instead of presenting our case we plead our case: "God, please, I'm begging You to do something." The problem with that is you're not bringing any evidence. You're just describing to God how you feel. If you're presenting your case as you would in a court of law, you come prepared and bring documents as evidence.

In the same way, when you go into the court of Heaven, so to speak, you've got to remind God what the contract says. "God, You said no weapon formed against me will prosper. Here's my evidence: Isaiah 54:17." "God, You said You are a very present help in my time of trouble. Here's my evidence: Psalm 46:1." When you go to God with evidence, with what He said, that's an unbeatable case.

*"Why do you complain to him that he responds to no one's words? For God does speak— now one way, now another . . ."*

JOB 33:13–14

# Rather Than Complain

I know a lady who was upset and at odds with her teenage daughter for several years. She often came to Lakewood to pray, but it seemed like she wasn't coming in to pray so much as to complain that God wasn't doing enough. I would try to convince her to keep believing. Instead of complaining to God, I told her to remind God of His promise: "Her children arise and call her blessed" (Proverbs 31:28).

Now, this woman's daughter was calling her every name except *blessed*. But still, the mother took it to heart. She presented her case, made her arguments, and brought forth her proof. About three years later, her daughter had a total change of heart. Today, the mother and daughter are best friends. That's what God wants to do in all of our lives.

## Distinguished

*Now Daniel so distinguished himself among the administrators and the satraps by his exceptional qualities that the king planned to set him over the whole kingdom.*

DANIEL 6:3

I have a friend who grew up in a family with a criminal reputation. As a young man, he gave his life to Christ and did his best to overcome all this negative baggage. But most people would have nothing to do with him. His name was like a badge of dishonor. I told him to remind God of His promises. "God, You said You would make my name great and distinguished. Genesis 12:2."

He went on to become a very successful coach. One day, he brought me a photograph in which he was accepting the Coach of the Year award in his school district. In his school lobby there is a plaque with the names of all of the winners of that award as "Distinguished Honorees," including his name. He smiled and said, "Joel, God has made my name distinguished."

## Present Your Case

*Know therefore that the LORD your God is God; he is the faithful God, keeping his covenant of love to a thousand generations of those who love him and keep his commandments.*

DEUTERONOMY 7:9

God is a faithful God. Don't plead your case. Present your case. Remind God what He said about you. Make a list of the promises you're standing on. When you go to the courtroom of Heaven, so to speak, take some evidence. Bring your proof. "God, You said I'm blessed and cannot be cursed." Present your case as my sister Lisa did: "God, You said You would make me the happy mother of children." "God, You said You would restore what the enemy has stolen."

Don't keep silent. Remind God again and again. Not begging God. No, go to Him in faith with a *You said*. If you put God in remembrance of His promises and do not put Him in remembrance of your problems, He will be faithful to His Word. What God promised, He will do.

## What You Believe

*"Have faith in God,"*
*Jesus answered.*

MARK 11:22

One of the greatest abilities God has given each of us is our ability to believe. If you believe, you can be successful. If you believe, you can overcome mistakes of the past. If you believe, you can fulfill your God-given destiny. There is incredible power in what we believe.

What you believe is greater than what the medical report says. What you believe is greater than what is in your bank account. I have a friend who came to this country with nothing but the clothes on his back. Today, he runs a Fortune 500 company. Against all odds, he believed he could do what God put in his heart. When you get in agreement with God and believe what He says about you, then what you believe can supersede any natural law.

*I also pray that you will understand the incredible greatness of God's power for us who believe him.*

EPHESIANS 1:19 NLT

## The Incredible Greatness

Notice in Paul's prayer for the Ephesian believers that the incredible greatness of God's power is activated only when we believe. That means right now the Creator of the universe is just waiting to release healing, restoration, favor, promotion, and abundance. The only catch is that we have to believe.

Sometimes, God will put a promise in your heart that seems impossible. God says your children will be mighty in the land. God says He will restore the years that were stolen. God says whatever you touch will prosper and succeed. It's easy to think, "It's never happening to me." But instead of talking yourself out of it, just respond with three simple words, "Lord, I believe." When you get in agreement with God, the incredible greatness of His power is activated.

## Just Believe

*Overhearing what they said, Jesus told him, "Don't be afraid; just believe."*

MARK 5:36

JULY

4

In the Scripture a man came to Jesus and said, "My little daughter is very sick. She is close to death. Will You come to my home and pray for her?" Jesus agreed, but along the way He kept getting stopped, one interruption after another. Finally word came back to Him saying, "No need to come. You've waited too late. The little girl has died." The people were very distraught, but Jesus said to them, "Don't be afraid; just believe."

Notice the phrase "just believe." Jesus went to the home, prayed for the little girl, and she came back to life. You, too, may be facing situations that seem impossible. But God is saying to you what He said to them: "If you will only believe, I will turn the situation around. If you just believe, breakthroughs are headed your way."

## Reprogram Your Computer

*Who is it that overcomes the world? Only the one who believes that Jesus is the Son of God.*

1 JOHN 5:5

God didn't say, "If you will pray three hours a day," or, "If you'll quote twelve chapters in the Scripture, I'll do it for you." No, He said, "Only the one who believes." In other words, if you will just get your mind going in the right direction and believe you can rise higher. Believe you can overcome the obstacle. Believe you can do something great and make your mark in this generation.

When you believe, the surpassing greatness of God's power is released. You may have to develop new habits. If you've been negative for a long time, you should retrain your thinking from "I can't" to "I can." From "It won't happen" to "It will happen." From "I'll never get well" to "God is restoring health unto me." Reprogram your computer. Load in some new software.

## Don't Be Intimidated

*"Be strong and courageous, and do the work. Do not be afraid or discouraged, for the LORD God, my God, is with you. He will not fail you or forsake you until all the work . . . is finished."*

1 CHRONICLES 28:20

When you believe, God will see to it that it's taken care of. When you believe, you have the Creator of the universe fighting your battles, arranging things in your favor, going before you, moving the wrong people out of the way. You couldn't have made it happen in your own strength, but because you are a believer, the surpassing greatness of God's power is at work in your life.

Now don't be intimidated by the size of the problem or the size of your dream. "Well, Joel, I was laid off, and you just don't know my financial situation." But I do know Jehovah Jireh; the Lord our provider. He is still on the Throne. One touch of God's favor and you'll go from barely making it to having more than enough.

*Finally, be strong in the Lord
and in his mighty power.*

EPHESIANS 6:10

## Unstoppable

If you have a medical situation that doesn't look good, know that the Lord our healer has not lost His power. If you have big dreams, but don't know the right people, know that God will bring the right people across your path. Realize that the bigger the problem, the bigger your destiny. The enemy would not be fighting you this hard unless he knew God had something amazing in your future. On the other side of that challenge is a new level of your destiny.

No disappointment. No setback. No injustice. No person. No hater. No jealousy can stand against our God. When you believe, all the forces of darkness cannot stop God from taking you where He wants you to go. Be a believer and not a doubter.

## He Is . . .

*But without faith it is impossible to please Him, for he who comes to God must believe that He is, and that He is a rewarder of those who diligently seek Him.*

### JULY
# 8

HEBREWS 11:6 NKJV

"When we come to God we must believe that He is." It doesn't really finish the Scripture. Believe that He is what? The passage leaves it open-ended. This is saying when you believe, God becomes whatever you need Him to be. He is strength when you're weak, healing when you're sick, favor when you need a good break, a way maker when you don't see a way, restoration when something has been stolen, vindication when you've been falsely accused. He is whatever you need Him to be.

You need to find out all that God means to be in your life. He is the God who can bring back to life what you thought was dead. He can do exceedingly, abundantly, above and beyond! He is a healer, a restorer, a God who gives beauty for ashes.

## See His Goodness

*For the word of the Lord
is right and true; he is
faithful in all he does.*

PSALM 33:4

A young couple heard me talking about how God wants to show us His unprecedented favor. For ten years they had worked hard, saved their funds, and now they dared to believe for the purchase of a house. They were about to close on a house they liked when the husband was laid off his job, and the house deal fell through. They were very disappointed, but they understood this principle: If you believe, you will see the goodness of God.

Five months later, the husband got a call from his old company. The old management team had been fired, and the new boss wanted him back. His job was restored as well as all of his benefits, all of his retirement, all of his seniority. And they found their dream house in a better neighborhood for a better price. God is a faithful God.

# It Will Be Well

*Tell the righteous it will be well with them . . .*

ISAIAH 3:10

You may go through some difficulties. You may endure hurts and disappointments, and people may do you wrong. But because you're a believer, it will be well with you. You lost your job, yes, but another job is coming. It will be well with you. The medical report doesn't look good, yes, but we have another report: It will be well with you.

You may have been praying, believing for your situation to change for a long time, but you don't see anything happening. Know that God is working behind the scenes right now arranging things in your favor. The answer is already on the way. God wants to give you a new beginning and bring you out better off than you were before. It's just a matter of time before it shows up. It will be well with you.

## Set Your Thermostat

*Look to the LORD and his strength; seek his face always.*

PSALM 105:4

I like to think that having faith is like setting the temperature on a thermostat. Now it may be 96 degrees in the room, but when you set the temperature to 72 degrees, you know it's just a matter of time before the temperature in the room matches the temperature that you've set.

In the same way, we should set our thermostats on what God says about us. God says you will lend and not borrow. Set your thermostat right there. Choose to believe. You may be far in debt at the moment, but don't be worried. As long as you've set your thermostat, as long as you keep believing, keep honoring God, keep being your best, you know it's just a matter of time before the conditions in your life match up to the conditions in your thinking.

## A Made-up Mind

*Rejoice always, pray continually, give thanks in all circumstances; for this is God's will for you in Christ Jesus.*

1 THESSALONIANS 5:16–18

God goes to work when He sees you have a made-up mind. Your thermostat is set on His promises, on faith, on restoration, on healing, on victory. It may not happen overnight, but God is faithful. He will do what He promised.

You may need to readjust your thermostat. At one time you believed you would do something great, start that business, beat that addiction, or meet the right person and get married. But it didn't happen on your timetable. You grew discouraged and gave up. God is saying, "Reset the thermostat." Start believing once again. Believe you can live free from pain. Believe you can move into that nicer home. Believe God is bringing the right people across your path. Keep the thermostat set. Have a made-up mind.

*For the Spirit God gave us does not make us timid, but gives us power, love and self-discipline.*

2 TIMOTHY 1:7

## Immovable

No matter how circumstances go in your life, stay in faith. Our attitude should be, "This is what God says about me. I am blessed. I will live and not die. My children will be mighty in the land. My latter days will be greater than my former days."

You may not see anything happening week after week, month after month, maybe even year after year. It doesn't matter. Your attitude is: "My thermostat is set. I'm not moved by what I see, by what I feel, by what people tell me. I'm moved by what I know. And I know when I believe, the incredible greatness of God's power is activated. I know when I believe, strongholds are broken. Favor, healing, promotion, and restoration are coming my way."

## Dead Bones Live

*. . . and I saw a great many bones on the floor of the valley, bones that were very dry. [The LORD] asked me, "Son of man, can these bones live?"*

EZEKIEL 37:2–3

JULY

# 14

Ezekiel was standing in a valley full of bones. Dead bones represent dreams and goals that we don't think will come to pass. God had the power to bring these bones to life, but He needed a person who believed, so He could work through him. God asked Ezekiel whether he believed or not. Ezekiel could have reasoned it out and said, "God, I don't see how that's going to happen." But Ezekiel shook off the doubt and said in effect, "Lord, I believe." The Spirit of God came on him. He started prophesying and somehow, some way, those dead bones came back to life.

Do you believe God can turn your situation around? Do you believe you can overcome past mistakes? When you get in agreement with God and believe, that allows God to release the incredible greatness of His power.

## "Even Now" Faith

*Jesus said to her, "I am the resurrection and the life. The one who believes in me will live, even though they die; and whoever lives by believing in me will never die. Do you believe this?"*

**JOHN 11:25–26**

Have you ever felt God showed up too late? You prayed, believed, stood on God's promises, but your prayers were not answered. That was the way Mary and Martha felt. Jesus had not come in time, and their brother, Lazarus, was dead. They were discouraged, depressed, and probably a little bit bitter. Jesus looked at them and said, "Take me to the place where you have laid him, the place where you stopped believing."

You have to go to that place in your life and ask yourself, "Is my God still on the Throne? Is my God still the God who is more than enough?" Sometimes you have to have "even now" faith where you say, "God, it looks impossible, but I know and believe even now You can turn it around." Your Lazarus can rise from the dead.

## Something Better

*Then Jesus said, "Did I not tell you that if you believe, you will see the glory of God?"*

JOHN 11:40

Mary and Martha at first were disappointed because Jesus didn't show up in time to heal Lazarus and that their prayers weren't answered in the way they wanted. But all along God knew what He was doing. He wasn't planning a healing. He was planning something better. He was planning a resurrection. Just because you believed and it didn't work out your way, or on your timetable, doesn't mean that it's over.

Sometimes God will wait on purpose not only so you know that it's His power, but so your doubters and your unbelieving relatives won't be able to deny that God has done something amazing in your life. God is planning something better. You believed, and you didn't get the promotion. You believed, and you didn't qualify for the new home. Keep believing. God has something better coming.

*For the vision is yet for an appointed time; but at the end it will speak, and it will not lie. Though it tarries, wait for it; because it will surely come, it will not tarry.*

HABAKKUK 2:3 NKJV

## Wait for It

Right now, behind the scenes God is working in your life, arranging things in your favor. Don't be intimidated by the size of what you are facing. Let this take root in your spirit. Because you are a believer, all will be well with you. All will be well with your family, with your finances, in your health, and with your career. You need to get ready, because God's promises are about to come to pass in your life. Stay in faith, and the Lord your God will make sure that it comes to pass.

It may not have happened in the past on your timetable. That's because it will be better, bigger, and greater than you've ever imagined. Be a believer. Take the limits off God. I declare you are going to see God's goodness in amazing ways!

## Uncommon Faith

*On the day the LORD gave the Amorites over to Israel, Joshua said to the LORD in the presence of Israel: "Sun, stand still over Gibeon, and you, moon, over the Valley of Aijalon."*

JOSHUA 10:12

One time Joshua was in the midst of a great battle. He and his men were trying to finish off this army, but the sun was going down. Joshua knew that if he couldn't get this army totally defeated, later on they would rise up and cause him problems. He could have easily got discouraged and thought, "It's not ever happening. Too bad for me."

But Joshua had uncommon faith. He was bold. So he asked God to stop the sun, something that had never been done before, and God did. When you have this uncommon faith, it brings a smile to God's face. God said in effect, "Joshua, if you're bold enough to ask it, I'm bold enough to do it." God interrupted the entire universe just because one man had uncommon faith.

## Boldness and Confidence

*When Jesus heard this, he was amazed and said to those following him, "Truly I tell you, I have not found anyone in Israel with such great faith."*

MATTHEW 8:10

Uncommon faith is not average faith. It's not ordinary. It's above and beyond. It gives you a boldness and a confidence to believe for the extraordinary. Average faith says, "God, help me to survive this recession." Uncommon faith says, "God, I believe You will prosper me right in the midst of this recession." Average faith says, "Maybe one day I'll get out of this problem. I don't know. It's pretty bad." Uncommon faith says, "I know I'm not only coming out, I'm coming out better off than I was before." When you have uncommon faith, you don't just believe to make your monthly house payment. You believe to totally pay off your house. You don't just ask God, "Help me to control my addiction." No, you ask God to totally set you free.

## Children of the Most High

*It is my pleasure to tell you about the miraculous signs and wonders that the Most High God has performed for me.*

DANIEL 4:2

Uncommon faith is radical faith. It's extreme. You believe God can do anything. You don't make little plans. You don't say, "God, just let me go as far as my parents did. Let me do as much as they did. Then I'll be okay. Then I'll be successful." Uncommon faith says, "God, give me a double portion. Let me do twice as much as those who went before me. Let me give twice as much. Let me have twice the influence, twice the wisdom, twice the friends, twice the creativity, and twice the income."

You may say, "Joel, that's kind of bold. Who do you think you are?" Here's who we are: We are children of the Most High God, full of uncommon faith.

*You are my hiding place;*
*you will protect me from*
*trouble and surround me*
*with songs of deliverance.*

PSALM 32:7

## The Hand of God

Have you ever asked God for something out of the ordinary? After my father went to be with the Lord, I was very concerned about keeping up our church attendance. I knew from years past that anytime it rained on Sunday mornings the crowds would be down. Every week I would pray that it would not rain during our Sunday morning services. I never told anyone but Victoria about my prayers, knowing other people would think that was extreme.

But for two years on the Sundays I was ministering, it might rain an hour before the service or two hours after the service, but it never once rained during those Sunday services. Some may think, "Oh, that's just a lucky break. That's just a coincidence." But I'm bold enough to believe that was the hand of God holding back the rain.

## Look Up

*Then the Lord took Abram out-side and said to him, "Look up into the sky and count the stars if you can. That's how many descendants you will have!"*

JULY

# 22

GENESIS 15:5 NLT

Raised in extreme poverty during the Great Depression, my father had no money, little education, no future to speak of. But at the age of seventeen, he gave his life to Christ. God put a dream in his heart that one day he would minister to people around the world. In the natural it looked totally impossible, but he had this uncommon faith to believe God would make it happen.

Years later, as we traveled together in India, in the jungles of Thailand, and along the Amazon River, I watched people recognize my father and hold up their Bibles and tell in their own language what they'd read in his books and heard him say on his tapes, videos, and television broadcasts. When all the odds were against him, my father saw God take him places that he never even dreamed of.

## Stretch Your Faith

*"Listen to me, Judah and people
of Jerusalem! Have faith in the
LORD your God and you will be
upheld; have faith in his proph-
ets and you will be successful."*

2 CHRONICLES 20:20

What is holding you back? It's easy to make
excuses: "I come from the wrong family. I
didn't get good breaks like you did." "I've had this
problem too long." "The economy is too down."
"I've made too many mistakes."

No, God knows how to get you to your desti-
nation. I want to light a new fire under you. There
is no obstacle too difficult for you to overcome.
No dreams put in your heart by God are too big
to accomplish. Ask yourself, "Is my faith radical? Is
what I'm believing for, the vision for my life, is it
big enough to make someone think, 'What's his
problem? Who does he think he is?'" If you are
not stretching your faith, you're not tapping in to
everything God has in store.

## Double Portion

*"Let me inherit a double portion of your spirit," Elisha replied. "You have asked a difficult thing," Elijah said, "yet if you see me . . ."*

2 KINGS 2:9–10

For years, Elisha was an assistant of the Prophet Elijah, who was very well known for the great miracles he performed and just for being a man of God. When Elijah grew very old and was about to go to Heaven, he asked Elisha what he wanted him to do for Elisha before he left. Elisha was thinking in uncommon ways when he asked for a double portion of Elisha's spirit.

Elijah responded, "Elisha, you have asked a difficult thing, yet . . ." That's the key word. He was saying, "It may be hard. You've asked for something big; nevertheless, it will happen. It is not too big for God." If you study Elisha's life, you'll find out that he did twice the miracles. He had a double portion of his anointing. We should ask for the same.

*Instead of your shame you will receive a double portion, and instead of disgrace you will rejoice in your inheritance. And so you will inherit a double portion in your land, and everlasting joy will be yours.*

ISAIAH 61:7 | **Increase**

When my father went to be with the Lord, people asked me, "Joel, do you think you can continue on what your dad and mom started?" I never said this arrogantly, but I would always tell them, "I don't think that I can just continue it. I believe that I can go further."

That's the way God intended it, for every generation to increase. It's interesting; the former sanctuary that my mom and dad built had eight thousand seats. The current Lakewood Church auditorium has sixteen thousand seats, exactly double. I'm not bragging. I'm simply making the case that if you take the limits off God and release your faith in uncommon ways, you will see God do uncommon things. God will increase you and take you further than previous generations.

## God Is Bigger

*"We went into the land to which you sent us, and it does flow with milk and honey!"*

NUMBERS 13:27

JULY

# 26

When Moses sent twelve men to spy out the Promised Land, ten came back and said, "We'll never defeat them. There are giants in the land." But the two other spies, Joshua and Caleb, came back with a different report. They said, "Yes, the people are big, but our God is bigger. We are well able to take the land. Let us go in at once."

Both groups saw the same giants and the same situation; the only difference was their perspective. One group focused on the size of their God; the other group focused on the size of their enemy. Out of the two million people camped next door to the Promised Land, only two made it in, Joshua and Caleb. Could it be that your perspective is keeping you from becoming all God's created you to be?

## Magnify the Lord

*Oh, magnify the Lord with me, and let us exalt His name together.*

**PSALM 34:3 NKJV**

What you focus on, you magnify. If you stay focused on your problem or what you don't have and how it will never work out, all you're doing is making it bigger than it really is. When you magnify something, you don't change the size of the object; you only change your perception of it. That was why David said, "Magnify the Lord with me."

When David faced Goliath, he never called him a giant. Everybody talked about his size, his strength, and his skill. But David called Goliath an uncircumcised Philistine. He never even gave him credit for being that big. Here's the key: David didn't deny it, but he didn't dwell on it. His attitude was: "I'm magnifying God's greatness. I'm not focusing on how big my problems are. I'm focusing on how big my God is."

## The Right Perspective

*"You come against me with sword and spear and javelin,*
*but I come against you in the name of the LORD Almighty,*
*the God of the armies of Israel, whom you have defied."*

1 SAMUEL 17:45

When David told his brothers and the other Israelites he wanted to fight Goliath, they said, "You can't fight him. You're just a kid. You don't have a chance." But David knew if God be for him, who would dare be against him? He knew he was strong in the Lord. David knew he wasn't alone, that all the forces of Heaven were backing him up. Others warned him, "David, Goliath is too big to hit." David said, "No, he's too big to miss."

He stood before Goliath and said, "You come against me with a sword and spear, but I come against you in the name of the Lord God of Israel!" David was magnifying his God. This teen-age boy—half the giant's size with no chance in the natural—defeated this huge giant. How? He had the right perspective.

## Can-Do Power

*Don't be intimidated in any way by your enemies.*

PHILIPPIANS 1:28 NLT

You may be up against a giant of debt, a giant of sickness, a giant legal problem. It looks impossible in the natural. But God is saying, "Don't be intimidated. Those for you are greater than those against you. Put your shoulders back and hold your head up high. You are not weak, defeated, or powerless. You are a child of the Most High God, anointed, equipped, well able. Don't you dare shrink back and think, 'It's just too big.'"

Get a new perspective. You are full of can-do power. The greatest force in the universe is breathing in your direction. The same power that raised Christ from the dead lives on inside of you. There is no challenge too tough for you, no enemy too big, no sickness too great, and no dream too far off.

## Coming Up Stronger

*And just as Christ was raised from the dead by the glorious power of the Father, now we also may live new lives.*

ROMANS 6:4 NLT

Do you know what made David king? Facing Goliath. When you face great difficulties, it's because God wants to take you to a higher level. Your challenge may have been meant for your harm, but God wants to use it to your advantage. That giant is not there to defeat you; it is there to promote you. You may be in tough times, but the right perspective is: "I'm not buried; I'm planted. I may be down, but I'm coming up stronger, better, increased, promoted, and at a new level."

I've found the size of your challenge is an indication of the size of your future. If you are facing a big giant challenge, don't be discouraged; that means God has something amazing just up in front of you. He has a new level of your destiny.

*But the more they were oppressed, the more they multiplied and spread; so the Egyptians came to dread the Israelites . . .*

EXODUS 1:12

## Bring on the Opposition

When the people of Israel dwelt in Egypt, it says, "The more opposition, the more they increased." When you face adversity, don't get depressed and say, "God, why is this happening to me? I thought Joel said this would be a good year. I went to church last Sunday."

Your attitude should be: "I know this opposition is a sign that increase is headed my way. It looks like a setback, but I know it's really a setup. It will not be a stumbling block to take me down. God will use it as a stepping-stone to take me up." You need to have an attitude of victory. Sometimes we're talking to God about how big our problems are, when we should be talking to our problems about how big our God is.

# Declare "I Will . . ."

*"This very day I will give the carcasses of the Philistine army to the birds and the wild animals, and the whole world will know that there is a God in Israel."*

1 SAMUEL 17:46

## AUGUST

# 1

I love the way David responded to Goliath when the giant was laughing and making fun of him for being so small. Goliath said, "Am I a dog that you would come at me with a stick?" David looked him in the eyes and said, "This very day I will give your carcass to the birds." He didn't say, "I hope so," "I believe so," or "I'm praying about."

Your declaration should be: "I will have a blessed year. I will beat this addiction. I will come out of debt. I will live healthy and strong. I will fulfill my God-given destiny." You may be up against big opposition, but don't be intimidated by that medical report, don't be intimidated by that legal situation, and don't be intimidated by the size of your dream.

*In him was life, and that life was the light of all mankind. The light shines in the darkness, and the darkness has not overcome it.*

JOHN 1:4–5

One of our Lakewood Church visitors told me she was in Houston for treatments, but she had such a positive attitude I found it hard to believe she was facing a serious illness. She told me, "Everything is fine," and she wouldn't even say the word *cancer*.

She would not give the disease credit for what it was. She wasn't denying it. She was choosing not to dwell on it. Her attitude was: "I'm not intimidated. This cancer is not bigger than my God. He made my body. He controls my destiny. No weapon formed against me will prosper. If it's not my time to go, I'm not going." She had the right perspective. She didn't let the disease define her or dominate her life.

**Not Afraid**

*God is our refuge and strength,*
*an ever-present help in trouble.*
*Therefore we will not fear . . .*

PSALM 46:1–2

I heard a story about a little boy who was try-ing to get his nerve up to stand up to a big bully. He was out in the front yard playing with his new telescope when his father came out and said, "No, son, you're doing it backward. Turn it around, and it will make everything bigger like it was meant to do." The little boy said, "I know that, Dad. But right now I'm looking at this bully. And when I look at him this way, it makes him so small that I'm not afraid of him anymore."

You may need to turn the telescope around. You've magnified your problem long enough. But if you'll turn it around, you'll see it from the right perspective; you'll realize it's nothing for God. All He has to do is breathe in your direction.

*For [Christ] must reign until he has put all his enemies under his feet.*

## Under Your Feet

1 CORINTHIANS 15:25

You need to see every obstacle, every sickness, every temptation, and every bad habit as being under your feet, because you are united to Jesus. It's no match for you. It's not permanent. It won't keep you from your destiny. It's already defeated, and it's just a matter of time before you walk it out.

That addiction won't dog you your whole life. It's under your feet. That depression in your family for so many years won't be passed to the next generation. It's under your feet. You're putting a stop to it. That struggle, lack, barely getting by, is not permanent. It won't keep you from being blessed. It's under your feet. It's just a matter of time before you break through to a new level. Keep the right perspective. It's under your feet.

## Look Down

*For we live by faith, not by sight.*

2 CORINTHIANS 5:7

David said in Psalm 59, "I will look down in triumph on all of my enemies." Notice he doesn't say "some of my enemies," but "all of my enemies." What am I going to do? "Look down in triumph." Why am I looking down? "Because they're under my feet."

You may be facing obstacles that don't feel like they're under your feet; that sickness seems big, that financial problem looks impossible, or maybe you've had the addiction for years. But you can't go by what you see. You should go by what you know. We walk by faith and not by sight. In the natural it may feel huge, but when you talk to that enemy as an act of faith, you need to do as David did and look down. It's under your feet.

## He Is Greater

*You, dear children, are from God and have
overcome them, because the one who is in you is
greater than the one who is in the world.*

1 JOHN 4:4

Sometimes before a big boxing match the two
fighters will come out at a press conference
and stand toe to toe, with their faces just two or
three inches apart. They'll stare each other in the
eye, trying to intimidate each other. They're saying, "I'm tougher, stronger, bigger, meaner. You're
not going to defeat me."

When you face an enemy, something's trying
to keep you from your destiny—a sickness, a bad
habit, an unfair situation. However, your enemy is
not at eye level. It may have a big bark and seem
larger and tougher, like you'll never defeat it. But
the truth is, it's no match for you. Look down. It's
under your feet. You are more than a conqueror.
If God be for you, who dare be against you? The
enemy has limited power, but our God has all
power.

## Power to Tread

*"Behold, I give unto you power to tread on serpents and scorpions, and over all the power of the enemy: and nothing shall by any means hurt you."*

LUKE 10:19 KJV

Now quit telling yourself, "I'll never get out of debt, never lose this weight, always struggle in this area." Change your perspective. You are not weak, defeated, or inferior. You are full of can-do power. The same spirit that raised Christ from the dead lives in you. You've got to start putting some things under your feet.

God said, "I've given you power to tread on all the power of the enemy." Notice that word *tread*. It has to do with a shoe. One translation says it means "to trample." If you'll start seeing those enemies as under your feet, as already defeated, you'll rise up with a new boldness and your faith will activate God's power in a new way.

*"No weapon formed against you will prevail . . ."*

ISAIAH 54:17

## It Won't Prevail

Isaiah doesn't say that you won't have difficulties. That's not realistic. It says challenges will come, people will talk, you may get a negative medical report, or a family member may get off course. God said the problem may form, but you can stay in peace, knowing that it won't prevail against you. That means it won't keep you from your destiny. Because you belong to Him, and because you dwell in the secret place, God has put a hedge of protection around you, a hedge of mercy, a hedge of favor that the enemy cannot cross.

When you're in difficulties and tempted to be upset, you need to remind yourself that no person, no sickness, no trouble, no bad break, and no disability can stop God's plan for your life. All the forces of darkness cannot keep you from your destiny.

## Positive and Hopeful

*The mind governed by the flesh is death, but the mind governed by the Spirit is life and peace.*

ROMANS 8:6

AUGUST

9

I read an article about scientists researching Alzheimer's disease. They studied the brains of those who had died with the disease and compared them to the brains of those who died without it. They found that many people had lesions on their brains that technically qualified them for having Alzheimer's, but the interesting thing was that when they were alive they showed no signs of Alzheimer's. Scientifically, they had it, but the symptoms never showed up. Their minds were sharp. Their memories were excellent.

The common denominator was that these people were positive and hopeful, and they stayed productive. We may have things that come against us because of our genetics, things that were passed down, but the good news is God can override it. God has the final say.

## The Deaf Hear

*"The blind receive sight, the lame walk, those who have leprosy are cleansed, the deaf hear, the dead are raised, and the good news is proclaimed to the poor."*

MATTHEW 11:5

Ramiro was born with no ears. The doctors told his parents he would never be able to hear or speak. However, Ramiro had parents who believed we serve a supernatural God. They knew they were armed with strength for the battle. They knew God put it under their feet. They just kept praying, believing, and speaking faith.

When Ramiro was a few months old, the doctors noticed that even though he didn't have ears, parts of his eardrums had formed. These incredibly gifted doctors performed a surgery to create ears for him and correct the problem. He got a little better, had more surgeries, and improved even more. Today, Ramiro can not only hear and speak, he can also sing. He leads worship for our young adults, and he appeared on *American Idol* singing "Amazing Grace" in front of millions of people.

## Glory Rises

*"Arise, shine, for your light has come, and the glory of the LORD rises upon you."*

ISAIAH 60:1

Whatever you're facing, it's under your feet. It's not permanent; it's temporary. The power that is for you is greater than any power that will be against you. Keep the right perspective. Don't focus on the size of the problem; focus on the size of your God. He's brought you through in the past, and He will bring you through in the future. The problem may have formed, but it will not prosper.

I speak strength into you. I speak healing, determination, new vision, favor, wisdom, courage. I declare you will not be intimidated. You are strong, confident, and well able. This is a new day. The tide of the battle is beginning to turn. You will be the overcomer. You will not be the victim; you are the victor. God will bring you out better off than you were before!

*. . . to comfort all who mourn, and provide for those who grieve in Zion—to bestow on them a crown of beauty instead of ashes, the oil of joy instead of mourning, and a garment of praise instead of a spirit of despair.*

ISAIAH 61:2–3

## Beauty for Ashes

It's easy to have a good attitude and pursue your dreams as long as everything is going your way. But what about the difficult times when a relationship doesn't work out, you get a bad health report, or a friend does you wrong? It's easy to lose your passion when you are hurting. Many people are sitting on the sidelines of life, nursing their wounds and not moving forward because of what they've been through.

You may have a *reason* to feel sorry for yourself, but you don't have a *right*. God promised to give you beauty for those ashes. He said He would pay you back double for the wrongs, but you have to do your part. If you are to see the beauty, if you're to get double, you have to shake off the self-pity.

## Play in Pain

*We are hard pressed on every side, but not crushed; perplexed, but not in despair; persecuted, but not abandoned; struck down, but not destroyed.*

AUGUST
# 13

2 CORINTHIANS 4:8–9

I was watching a football game in which a big offensive lineman had a broken hand and bruised ribs. The trainers wanted him to sit out, but he refused to miss the game. He had a big cast on his arm and was wearing a special vest to protect his ribs. A reporter asked him how he felt: "It's a little painful, but I'd rather be in the game in pain than sitting on the sidelines watching."

We all have wounds, but you can't let a loss, a health issue, or a divorce be your excuse to sit on the sidelines. Sometimes in life you have to play in pain. Bandage what's hurting. Forgive the person who did you wrong. Shake off the discouragement, let go of what didn't work out, and get back in the game.

## Stay in the Game

*I consider that our present
suffering are not worth
comparing with the glory
that will be revealed in us.*

**ROMANS 8:18**

I said in passing to an older woman who very
faithfully attends our church services, "I haven't
seen you lately. Where've you been?" She said,
"Joel, I had an emergency surgery and was In the
hospital for three months." "Wow! We're so glad
to have you back," I said. "How are you doing?" For
as long as I live I will never forget her words. She
said, "I'm hurting, but I'm here."

That's the kind of people God rewards. Faithful people. People who are determined. People
who get knocked down, but don't stay down.
Instead, they get back up again. You can't let the
hurt, the pain, or the bad break cause you to be
bitter, to lose your passion, or to start blaming
God. You need to stay in the game.

## Hang in There

*Those the Lord has rescued will return. They will*
*enter Zion with singing; everlasting joy will crown*
*their heads. Gladness and joy will overtake them,*
*and sorrow and sighing will flee away.*

ISAIAH 51:11

Anybody can sit on the sidelines. Anybody can find an excuse to be sour, to drop out, or to give up on life. When you're hurting and in pain, it's easy to become fixated on your hurt, your disappointments, or your bad breaks. All that will do is bring more discouragement, more self-pity, eventually even depression.

You need to make up your mind to stay in the game. You can't just be faithful only as long as you feel perfectly well, as long as everybody treats you right, or as long as it's sunny and cool outside. No matter what life deals your way, your attitude should be: "I'm hurting, but I'm still here. A friend did me wrong, but I'm still here. Business is slow, but I'm still here. I didn't feel like coming, but I'm still here."

## Sow Seeds

*Those who go out weeping, carrying seed to sow,*
*will return with songs of joy, carrying sheaves with them.*

PSALM 126:6

In 1981, my mother was diagnosed with terminal liver cancer and given a few weeks to live. She had a good reason to be discouraged. She could have gone home, pulled the curtains, and been depressed. But my mother stayed in the game. She would drive across town to pray for a sick friend and come to church every weekend and pray for other people in need. The truth is she needed prayer more than they did, but she was sowing seeds.

One of the best things you can do when you're hurting is go out and help somebody else who is hurting. Get your mind off your problems and pain by helping somebody else in need. When you help others in your time of need, you are sowing a seed God can use to change your situation.

### Scars to Stars

*In her deep anguish Hannah prayed to the L ORD, weeping bitterly. . . . Eli answered, "Go in peace, and may the God of Israel grant you what you have asked of him."*

1 SAMUEL 1:10, 17

When my sister Lisa was in her early twenties, she went through a devastating unwanted divorce. It was an unfair situation. For weeks she was so depressed that she wouldn't leave the house and felt like she was having a nervous breakdown. Our family tried but could not cheer her up. Finally, a minister friend, T. L. Osborn, called Lisa and said, "You know I love you, but you've got to quit feeling sorry for yourself. If you'll move forward, God will take your scars and turn them into stars for His glory."

When Lisa heard that, it's like a stronghold was broken in her mind. She started to reach out to other people who were hurting. Today, more than twenty years later, she's happily married, with a great husband and three beautiful children. God gave her beauty for those ashes.

*"Rise up; this matter is in your hands. We will support you, so take courage and do it."*

EZRA 10:4

### New Life

When you've been hurt, the Prophet Isaiah says, "Arise from the depression in which the circumstances have kept you. Rise to a new life." Notice, if you want a new life, you can't sit back in self-pity. You can't wait until all your wounds heal and you feel 100 percent. You've got to arise from that discouragement.

Shake off what didn't work out. Quit mourning over what you've lost. Quit dwelling on who hurt you and how unfair it was, and rise to a new life. When God sees you show up with the attitude: "I'm hurting, but I'm still here. I'm hurting, but I know God is still on the Throne. I'm hurting, but I'm expecting God to turn it around"—that's when He goes to work. That's when God will pay you back for the wrongs that have happened to you.

## Run with Perseverance

*And let us run with perseverance the race marked out for us, fixing our eyes on Jesus, the pioneer and perfecter of faith.*

HEBREWS 12:1–2

AUGUST

# 19

If you're experiencing a tough time, stay in the game. If a friend betrayed you, go out and find some new friends. The right people are in your future. If you lost your job, go out and find another job. When one door closes, God will always open another door. If you're fighting a sickness, don't start planning your funeral. Arise.

When God sees you do your part, He will do His part. He will give you a new life. He will restore your health, give you new opportunities, new relationships. He will give you a new perspective. A painful time is not the end. Even though it was unfair, it is not over. There is still life after the sickness, life after the divorce, and life after the bad break. A full life is still in front of you.

# Our Redeemer Lives

*"I know that my redeemer lives, and that in the end he will stand on the earth."*

JOB 19:25

The Scripture says Job went through unthinkably tough times. Everything that could go wrong did—the loss of his wealth, his children, and his health. He was tempted to give up on life. But in the midst of that pain, Job said, "I know my Redeemer lives." He was saying in effect, "I'm hurting, but I'm still in the game. I'm hurting, but I know my God is still on the Throne."

When Job came through that challenge, God not only brought him out; God paid him back double for what he lost. After the trouble, after the loss, after the sickness, after the business went down, his life still was not over. He didn't end on a sour, defeated note. He went on to live a blessed, happy 140 years, enjoying his grandchildren, accomplishing his dreams, fulfilling his destiny.

## A Full Life

*"They will be like a tree planted by the water that sends out its roots by the stream. It does not fear when heat comes; its leaves are always green."*

JEREMIAH 17:8

Your life is not over because you had a set-back. God has an "after this" in your future. When you go through tough times, don't be surprised if the enemy doesn't whisper in your ear, "You'll never be as happy as you used to be. You've seen your best days. This setback is the end of you." Let that go in one ear and out the other.

God is saying to you that after the cancer, after the bad break, after the disappointment, there is still a full life. If you stay in the game and do not grow bitter, God will bring you out. You have not danced your best dance. You have not laughed your best laugh. You have not dreamed your best dream. He will bring you out with double what you had before.

*Let love and faithfulness never leave you; . . . write them on the tablet of your heart. Then you will win favor and a good name in the sight of God and man.*

PROVERBS 3:3–4

## Win Favor

A pro football player's younger brother was tragically killed in an accident the day before a big game. This player practically raised his siblings. You can imagine the pain and shock he must have been in. The coach told him to go home and spend as much time as he needed with his family. But he said, "No, Coach. I'm playing in the game tomorrow in memory of my brother. That's what he would want me to do."

It's interesting; this player had one of the greatest games of his career. Some people would see it as a coincidence, just the adrenaline of the moment. But I see it as the hand of God. I believe God was saying, "If you'll dare stay in the game, if you'll dare play with pain, I'll breathe My favor on your life."

## Wipe Away the Tears

*Then David got up from the ground. After he
had washed, put on lotions and changed his clothes,
he went into the house of the LORD and worshiped.*

2 SAMUEL 12:20

Nobody would fault you for being discouraged when you are nursing your wounds over a lost loved one, a serious illness, a child with special needs, or a legal battle. That's what most people expect. But when you defy the odds and say, "Hey, I'm hurting, but I'm still here," the most powerful force in the universe breathes in your direction.

You may be in a difficult time. You could easily be discouraged. But God is saying, "It's time to wipe away the tears. Wash your face. Put on a new attitude and get back in the game." You may not be able to do what you used to. You may have some aches and some limitations. That's all right. God is not necessarily concerned about your performance. He is looking at the fact that you're in the game.

### Still on the Throne

*The God of peace will soon crush Satan under your feet.*
*The grace of our Lord Jesus be with you.*

ROMANS 16:20

You were treated badly. It takes an act of faith to ignore the voices giving you excuses to sit on the sidelines. When you refuse to listen to them and get back in the game, God sees your effort. God knows what it took for you to come to church or to reach out to someone else in need.

Others may not know the battles you had to fight to get back in the game. They see all the opportunities you had to get sour and throw in the towel. Just the fact that you showed up says to God, "You are still on the Throne." You're saying to yourself, "I'm in it for the long haul." And you're saying to the enemy, "You're under my feet. There's nothing you can do to keep me from my destiny."

### He Feels Our Pain

*For we have not an high priest which cannot be touched with the feeling of our infirmities; but was in all points tempted like as we are, yet without sin.*

HEBREWS 4:15 KJV

When Jesus was here on this earth, He felt every pain, every emotion, that we would ever feel. He knows what it's like to be lonely, to go through a loss, to be betrayed, or to be discouraged—so much so that He sweated great drops of blood. He's been where we are. The Scripture says, "He is touched with the feeling of our infirmities."

When you hurt, God feels the pain. You're His most prized possession. You're His child. When you arise in spite of the pain and get in the game, that's the seed God will use to take the scar and turn it into a star.

> *As you know, we count as blessed those who have perse-vered. You have heard of Job's perseverance and have seen what the Lord finally brought about. The Lord is full of compassion and mercy.*

**JAMES 5:11**

## Get God's Attention

A younger man who always has a smile and never misses our church services came up for prayer one Sunday. He rolled up his sleeve. His whole arm was red. It looked like somebody had taken an ice pick to it. What I didn't realize is that he had been on dialysis for twelve years. All this time he seemed as happy as could be, but he was hurting and playing in pain. That gets God's attention in a great, great way.

About three months ago this man received a kidney transplant from a friend. Today, he's healthy, free from that pain. After the struggle, after the pain, there was still a bright future in front of him. Because he stayed in the game, he came into his "after this." God will do the same thing for you.

## "After This"

*But Ruth replied, "Don't urge me to leave you or to turn back from you. Where you go I will go, and where you stay I will stay. Your people will be my people and your God my God."*

RUTH 1:16

Ruth was still a young lady when her husband died. She could have easily given in to self-pity, but Ruth stayed in the game, choosing instead to care for her mother-in-law, Naomi, who was widowed and in need. One day Ruth was out working in the field and met Boaz, the owner of all the fields in that area. They fell in love, got married, and became the great-grandparents of King David, one of the greatest men to ever live.

Ruth could have sat on the sidelines the rest of her life after her loss, but she understood this principle: She played in pain. She was injured, but she kept doing the right thing. God had an "after this" for Ruth. After the loss, after the pain, God said, "I'll give you an ancestor who will change the world."

# AUGUST
# 28

*Then the LORD said to Moses,
"Why are you crying out to me?
Tell the Israelites to move on."*

**EXODUS 14:15**

Y ou may be in pain today. Maybe you've suffered a loss, been through a disappointment.
My message is, "That is not the end. God still has
a plan." Don't sit around nursing your wounds.
Don't let bitterness and discouragement set
the tone for your life. God is saying, "Arise. Wipe
away the tears and get back in the game." Have
the attitude: "I'm hurting, but I'm still here. I'm disappointed, but I've still got a smile. They did me
wrong, but I'm still giving God praise."

If you will stay in the game, God will always
have an "after this" for you. I believe and declare,
in spite of the pain, in spite of the adversity,
because you're still in the game, God is going to
make the rest of your life the best of your life.

**Come to Jesus**

*"Come to me, all you who are weary and burdened, and I will give you rest. Take my yoke upon you and learn from me, for I am gentle and humble in heart, and you will find rest for your souls."*

MATTHEW 11:28–29

What do you do when one of life's battles has lasted longer than you thought it would? You've prayed. You've believed. You've done what you're supposed to, but you're still waiting to meet the right person. Or you're still looking for the right job. Or you're still praying that a child you care about will get back on track.

We all grow tired sometimes, tired of trying to make a business grow, tired of dealing with a sickness, tired of raising a difficult child, tired of being lonely and waiting to meet the right person. We can even be doing what we love, whether it's living in the house of our dreams, raising great children, or working at a good job, but if we're not careful, we can lose our passion and allow weariness to set in.

*And let us not be weary in well doing: for in due season we shall reap, if we faint not.*

GALATIANS 6:9 KJV

## Faint Not

The word *weary* means "to lose the sense of pleasure, to not feel the enjoyment that you once felt." The problem is when you allow yourself to become weary, you'll be tempted to quit: to quit growing, to quit standing for that wayward child, to quit believing that you'll become healthy and whole, or to quit pursuing your goals and dreams.

Two words are the key to this whole passage—*faint not*. In other words, if you don't give up, if you shake off the weariness, if you put on a new attitude knowing that God is still in control, if you dig your heels in and say, "This too shall pass. I know it's not permanent. I've come too far to stop now," if you "faint not," you will see the promise come to pass.

# The Weariness Test

*. . . yet I will rejoice in the LORD,*
*I will be joyful in God my Savior.*
*The Sovereign LORD is my*
*strength; he makes my feet like*
*the feet of a deer, he enables*
*me to tread on the heights.*

AUGUST
# 31

HABAKKUK 3:18–19

A woman visiting our church told me that she was in town for a checkup at the big cancer center in Houston, and she hadn't received the news she'd hoped for. She'd gone through six months of chemotherapy. She was hoping she was done, of course. She found out that the chemo did do some good, but they told her she needed another six months of treatments. She was so disappointed. She said, "Joel, I'm tired. I don't think I can do this for six more months."

On the way to our victories we will always face the weariness test. We will be tempted to become discouraged and give up. The test never comes when we're fresh. It never comes when we first start out. It always comes when we're tired. That's when we're the most vulnerable.

## When Weariness Sets In

*But the men who had gone up with him said, "We can't attack those people; they are stronger than we are."*

NUMBERS 13:31

The people of Israel had gone through the wilderness, overcoming obstacles, defeating all kinds of enemies. They were next door to the Promised Land, which God had already said He would give them. All they had to do was go in and fight for it. But they allowed weariness to set in, and weariness leads to discouragement.

When you're discouraged, you see the problem instead of the possibility. You talk about the way it is instead of the way it can become. The people of Israel started complaining: "Moses, our enemy is too big. We'll never defeat them." They made a permanent decision based on a temporary feeling. If you allow yourself to become weary and you lose your passion, you, too, will be tempted to make decisions based on how you feel rather than based on what you know.

## Words of Faith

*"You wearied yourself by such going about,*
*but you would not say, 'It is hopeless.' You found renewal*
*of your strength, and so you did not faint."*

ISAIAH 57:10

When we feel weary, too often we think, "I can't take this anymore. I'm so tired. It's just too hard." Yet, the more you talk about how tired you are, the more tired you become. You're just adding fuel to the fire. Don't talk about the way you are. Talk about the way you want to be.

You need to have words of faith and victory coming out of your mouth. In other words, "This may be hard, but I know I'm well able. God, You said You have armed me with strength for every battle. You said I can do all things through Christ who infuses inner strength into me. I'm equipped. I'm empowered. I am strong in the Lord." If you talk to yourself the right way, you will feel the second wind kick in.

## Mount Up with Wings

*But those who wait on the L*ORD *shall renew their strength;*
*they shall mount up with wings like eagles, they shall run*
*and not be weary, they shall walk and not faint.*

ISAIAH 40:31 NKJV

We all become weary. In fact, if you never feel like giving up, your dreams and goals are too small. When the pressure comes to be discouraged and to think you can't take it anymore, that is completely normal. Every person feels that way at times.

Isaiah gives us the solution. He said in effect: "This is a way to get your second wind and have your strength renewed. Wait on, or hope in, the Lord." That doesn't mean to sit around and be passive, complacent. It means to wait with expectancy, not complaining, not discouraged, not talking about all the reasons why it won't work out. The right way to wait is by saying, "Father, thank You that the answer is on the way. You are bigger than these obstacles. Thank You that You are bringing my dreams to pass."

## Catch Your Second Wind

> *I said, "Oh, that I had the wings of a dove! I would fly away and be at rest."*
>
> PSALM 55:6

You may be up against major obstacles. Perhaps some of it is the result of your own mistakes. When you look out into your future, it can be very overwhelming. You can't see how you will make it.

When you give God praise, you talk about His greatness; you go through the day expecting Him to turn it around. God promises He will renew your strength. The Scripture says, "You will run and not get weary." This is a reference to catching your second wind. That's God breathing strength, energy, passion, vision, and vitality back into your spirit. You won't just come out the way you were. You will come out on wings like eagles. You will come out stronger, higher, better off than you were before.

> *This is the day the Lord has made; we will rejoice and be glad in it.*
>
> PSALM 118:24 NKJV

## Strength for Today

I know a woman who raised her children and got them off to college. She was looking forward to this new season in her life. But because of unusual circumstances, she has had to raise her grandson, who is just a toddler. Of course she loves her grandbaby, but she said, "Joel, I don't think I can do this again. Another fifteen years? I don't think I have the strength to make it."

I told her she can't focus fifteen years down the road. If she looks that far out, she will be overwhelmed. You have to take it one day at a time. You don't have the strength you need for tomorrow. When you get to tomorrow, you'll have the strength for that day. God asks only: "Will you do it today? Will you take hold of My strength today?"

## Do Not Worry

*"Therefore do not worry about tomorrow, for tomorrow will worry about itself. Each day has enough trouble of its own."*

MATTHEW 6:34

# SEPTEMBER
## 6

If you are caught in worry—"How am I going to make it next week, or next month, or twenty years from now?"—that worry will drain your strength, energy, passion, and victory. All worry does is weigh us down and keep us from enjoying life.

Instead of worrying about your future, say to yourself, "I can do this one more day. I may not know how I can do it the next week, but I can do it for twenty-four more hours. I can stay in faith and keep a good attitude one more day. I can have a smile on my face twenty-four more hours." If you will pass the test today, then when you get to tomorrow, the strength you need for that day will be there. Take it a day at a time.

## One More Step

*Do you not know that in a race all the runners run, but only one gets the prize? Run in such a way as to get the prize.*

1 CORINTHIANS 9:24

I like to exercise to stay fit. Sometimes when I am out running, I get tired. Those thoughts start coming, saying, "You need to stop. It's hard, and look at how far you've got to go."

The real battle takes place in our minds. If I dwell on those thoughts and start thinking about how I feel and how many hills there are and how far I've got to go, I'll stop. Instead, I quit looking at the distance and just start telling myself, "I can do this one more step. One more step. One more step." When I focus on the next step, I press past the pain, find a rhythm, and all of a sudden my second wind kicks in, and instead of barely making it, I'm mounting up on those wings like eagles. I'm finishing strong.

## The End Date

*"A person's days are determined; you have decreed the number of his months and have set limits he cannot exceed."*

JOB 14:5

Thoughts will come to you: "This situation is never changing. You're never getting well. You're never reaching your goals." But don't listen to them. God has set an end date for the trouble, the struggle, the sickness, the addiction, or the loneliness.

Remind yourself of that when you're in a difficult season and you feel the weariness creeping in, telling you, "It's not worth it. You've got too far to go." Tell yourself, "God has set an end to this loneliness. I won't always struggle in my finances. I won't always be fighting these addictions and bad habits. Jehovah Rapha, the Lord my healer, has set an end to this sickness." Stand strong. Keep believing. Keep being your best. If you stay on track and do what's right, you will see the end come to pass.

*"You armed me with strength for battle . . ."*

2 SAMUEL 22:40

## Strength for Battle

I know you're not a fainter. You are strong! You are a warrior, a victor and not a victim. When life gets tough, remind yourself that God has armed you with strength for every battle. You are full of can-do power. Don't go around feeling weak and defeated and like you can't take it anymore. If it was too much for you, God wouldn't have allowed it.

Instead of complaining, tell yourself, "I can handle this." Put your shoulders back, look those obstacles in the eye, and say: "You're no match for me. I know your end has already been set, and it's just a matter of time before God turns it around. It's just a matter of time before He brings that dream to pass."

## Abundance of Grace

*And God is able to bless you abundantly,
so that in all things at all times, having all that you need,
you will abound in every good work.*

2 CORINTHIANS 9:8

A friend of mine is in the military, and he had just found out he would be deployed overseas for one year. He and his wife and two small children had never been apart for an extended time. His wife was very worried and wondered how she was going to make it.

I told her what I'm telling you: Your challenge may be difficult, but you can handle it. God has given you the grace for this season. If you weren't up to this, God wouldn't have brought it across your path. In tough times remind yourself there is always a reward for doing right. God never fails to compensate you. He pays very well. The season may be difficult right now, but if you keep doing the right thing, get ready—the reward is coming.

## On the Verge

*Keep thy heart with all diligence;*
*for out of it are the issues of life.*

**PROVERBS 4:23** KJV

You may be camped next to the Promised Land like the people of Israel, on the verge of stepping to a new level of God's favor, but you're tired. The battle has taken longer than you expected. You stand at a crossroads. You can either let that weariness weigh you down, causing you to give up and settle where you are, or you can dig your heels in and say, "I've come too far to stop now. I'll keep pursuing my goals. I'll keep hoping, praying, stretching, growing."

When you have that kind of attitude, you will feel your second wind kick in. I've learned this: You face the greatest pressure when you are close to your victory. When the intensity has been turned up, that's a sign you're about to step to a new level of God's favor.

**A New Season**

*"I will send down showers in season; there will be showers of blessing."*

EZEKIEL 34:26

I can sense in my spirit the season is changing. The depression is coming to an end and joy is about to break forth. Your lack and struggle is coming to an end and a new season of increase, promotion, and more than enough is coming your way. If you've had constant medical problems and not felt up to par, that is coming to an end. A season of health, wholeness, and vitality is coming your way.

Press past the pain and discomfort. Press past the feelings telling you to settle. Press past the weariness. Get your fire back. You have not seen your best days. Your greatest victories are still out in front of you. Those adversities and struggles will not go to waste; God is using them to prepare you for the amazing future He has in store.

*As iron sharpens iron, so one man sharpens another.*

PROVERBS 27:17

## Increased Endurance

When I ran track in high school, our coach gave us unbelievable workouts. One time we had to run a half a mile, take a two-minute break, and then run the next one—eighteen times in a row. We thought, "He's trying to kill us." But several months later, we were all running at new levels and breaking our old records, and we realized he was simply increasing our endurance. He was stretching us so we could reach our full potential.

In the same way God sometimes will allow us to face difficulties to increase our endurance, to stretch us so we can reach our full potential. When you make it through, you will not only receive your reward, you also will have an inner strength, a confidence, and a resolve you never had before.

# Strength to Conquer

*"Hear, O Israel: Today you are on the verge of battle with your enemies. Do not let your heart faint, do not be afraid, and do not tremble or be terrified because of them . . ."*

DEUTERONOMY 20:3 NKJV

## SEPTEMBER
# 14

You will face situations today that might have been too much ten years ago. They might have caused you to be upset and fall apart. But because you've passed these tests, something has been deposited inside your spirit. What used to be a big deal is not a big deal at all.

What's happening? You're growing. You're increasing. You're stepping up to new levels. I believe right now the Creator of the universe is breathing a second wind into you. Just receive it by faith. Strength is coming into your body. Strength is coming into your mind. You will run and not grow weary. You will walk and not faint. You will not drag through life defeated or depressed. You will soar through life on wings like eagles!

## Open and Closed Doors

*"These are the words of him who is holy and true, who holds the key of David. What he opens no one can shut, and what he shuts no one can open."*

REVELATION 3:7

We all know that God opens doors. We've seen Him give us favor, good breaks, promotion. That's the hand of God opening the door. But the same God who opens doors will close doors. Maybe you prayed, but you didn't get a promotion you wanted. You applied, but your loan application didn't go through. A relationship you'd enjoyed didn't work out. So often we can become discouraged and feel like God has let us down.

But God can see the big picture for your life. God knows where every road is leading. He knows the dead ends. He can see the shortcuts. He knows some roads are a big circle. A big part of faith is trusting God when you don't understand why things happen the way they do.

## Always for Good

*And we know that in all things God works for the good of those who love him, who have been called according to his purpose.*

ROMANS 8:28

We can't see what God can see. God may close a door because you're believing too small. If He opened the door, it would limit what He wants to do in your life. Another door may close because it's not the right time, or there are other people involved and they're not ready yet. If God opened that door at the wrong time, it wouldn't work out.

The bottom line is: God has your best interests at heart. When a door closes, you don't know what God is saving you from. If your prayers aren't answered the way you want, instead of being discouraged or feeling like God let you down, why don't you have a bigger perspective? The reason the door closed is because God has something better in store.

*. . . the Lord knows how to
rescue the godly from trials . . .*

**2 PETER 2:9**

# If God Wanted

It's no accident that some doors are closed to you. You may not understand why right now. But if God wanted you to have that promotion you didn't get, He would have given it to you. Shake off the disappointment and move forward. Know that there is something better coming. Or if God wanted the person who left you to stay, that person would still be with you. Shake it off. The right people are in your future.

You may feel that the opportunity of a lifetime just passed you by. But one day you will look back and thank God for the closed door, because if God hadn't closed the door, you wouldn't have met the right person, or you would have been stuck at one level and not seen the amazing favor He has in your future.

## His Way

*Three times I pleaded with the Lord to take it away from me. But he said to me, "My grace is sufficient for you, for my power is made perfect in weakness."*

2 CORINTHIANS 12:8–9

# SEPTEMBER
# 18

I used to get excited about my open doors, but I really felt down about my closed doors. Now I thank God for my closed doors just as much as I do my open doors. I want you to come to this place where you are so confident that God is directing your steps, you say, like David: "God, my life is in Your hands."

If you believe that, then when a door closes and you don't get your way, you won't be upset. Your attitude will be: "God closed this door on purpose, and what God closes I don't want to open. I don't want my way. I want His way." That's a very freeing way to live. When you really believe God is in complete control, it takes all the pressure off.

*I am not saying this because I am in need, for I have learned to be content whatever the circumstances.*

PHILIPPIANS 4:11

God knows what He is doing. If He wants a door to open, you can be certain it will open. So when you pray and believe in faith, if the door doesn't open, take it as a sign from God. It's not His best. Sometimes, you may be disappointed, but God loves you too much to open that door. God is not letting you down. He is doing you a favor. He is keeping you from all kinds of heartache and pain.

Be content with the answer God gives you. Put the dream on the altar and say, "God, if this is Your best for my life, I trust You. If it happens, I will be happy and thank You for it. If it doesn't work out, I won't be discouraged. I know that means You have something better in store."

## Much Bigger

*"Take possession of the land and settle in it,
for I have given you the land to possess."*

NUMBERS 33:53

When I took over the ministry at Lakewood Church, we needed property to build a new sanctuary. We found a perfect hundred-acre tract of land that had been on the market for more than twenty years. But the morning we went in to negotiate, we were told the property had been sold the previous night. I was so disappointed, but I thought, "God is still on the Throne. He has the final say."

When I heard that the Compaq Center was up for sale, I knew that was the reason God closed the other door. It was too small. It would have limited what God wanted to do. Things fell into place, and now we have an amazing home in the former Compaq Center. This was exceedingly, abundantly, above and beyond. God's dream for our lives is so much bigger than our own dreams.

## Stay Faithful

*"For the eyes of the LORD range throughout the earth to strengthen those whose hearts are fully committed to him."*

### 2 CHRONICLES 16:9

There will be times when a door closes and you can't understand why. In a relationship, you may feel that you'd found the perfect person, but it doesn't work out. Or maybe it will be the perfect house, but your offer will be turned down. It may not make sense when it happens, but one day it will.

Here's the question: Will you stay in faith while you wait to see what God is up to? Will you not grow discouraged and start complaining? "Nothing good ever happens to me. I can't believe I didn't get the promotion." Or, "I treated this girl like a queen and she just wants to be friends. God, I want to be a husband!" Be patient. Trust God with your life. He knows what He is doing.

## Trust Him

*Trust in the L*ORD *with all your heart and lean not on your own understanding; in all your ways submit to him, and he will make your paths straight.*

PROVERBS 3:5–6

I've learned the closed doors in life are just as important as the open doors. You know what brought Lakewood Church to the former stadium location? A closed door. Don't be discouraged by your closed doors. You may want a piece of property right now, but God has a building already built for you. He has more than you can ask or think—an exceedingly, abundantly, above-and-beyond future.

God loves you so much that He hasn't answered certain prayers. He hasn't allowed certain people into your life whom you really wanted, because they would have limited your growth. Learn to trust Him. Thank Him for your open doors. Celebrate His goodness. But thank Him just as much for your closed doors, knowing that He is still directing your steps.

> *"For my thoughts are not your thoughts, neither are your ways my ways,"* declares the LORD. *"As the heavens are higher than the earth, so are my ways higher than your ways and my thoughts than your thoughts."*

ISAIAH 55:8–9

## More Rewarding

A hurting young lady came for prayer. Her boyfriend had broken up with her, and she didn't think she could live without him. Month after month she prayed that the relationship would be restored, but he ended up marrying someone else. She was so discouraged that she dropped out of church. Several years later, however, she came to church with a handsome husband by her side and a beautiful daughter and said, "I thank God every day that He didn't answer my prayer." The other fellow had been married and divorced two times and constantly in and out of trouble.

Let these words sink down into your spirit: God's way is better than your way. His plan is bigger than your plan. His dream for your life is more rewarding, more fulfilling, better than you've ever dreamed.

## Pass the Test

*I have chosen the way of faithfulness; I have set my heart on your laws.*

PSALM 119:30

SEPTEMBER

# 24

When you want something so badly that you convince yourself you can't live without it, you try to make it happen. You may pray night and day for it, but God is so merciful if it's not His best that He is not going to answer that prayer. He loves you too much to open that door. Why don't you trust Him? He wants you to fulfill your destiny more than you do. He is in complete control.

When you come to a closed door, consider it a test of your faith. Will you become bitter, live in self-pity, and give up on your dreams, or will you move forward knowing that God is still in control? If you pass the test, God will release what He has in your future. And many times it will be exactly what you're praying for.

## Trust and Obey

*Then God said, "Take your son, your only son, whom you love—Isaac—and go to the region of Moriah. Sacrifice him there as a burnt offering on a mountain I will show you."*

GENESIS 22:2

God instructed Abraham to put his son Isaac, the person who meant the most to him, on the altar as a sacrifice. Since the Lord was directing his steps, Abraham didn't try to figure out why He made this request. Just when Abraham was going to harm him, God said, "No, Abraham. Don't do it. I just wanted to see if you trusted Me enough to give Me your own son."

Abraham passed the test. What happened? God gave him back what he really wanted, the person who meant so much to him. When you face a disappointment, or a closed door, or when your plans don't work out, if you keep a good attitude and stay in faith, you will pass the test. If you do that, it allows God to give back to you what you really want the most.

### Things You Won't Understand

*The LORD directs our steps, so why try to understand everything along the way?*

PROVERBS 20:24 NLT

I f you're trying to figure out everything that doesn't go your way, you'll become confused and frustrated. "God, why didn't I get that job I applied for? It's perfect for me." You could find freedom if you would just quit trying to figure out everything. Let it go and move forward.

God can see things you can't see. It may not make sense right now, but one day when God's whole plan unfolds, you will see what God was up to. A part of trusting is saying, "God, I don't understand it. It doesn't seem fair. But God, I believe that You order my steps and my stops. I know just as You can close doors, You will open them. So I'm keeping a good attitude. I'm moving forward in faith knowing that You have my best interests at heart."

*For now we see only a reflection as in a mirror; then we shall see face to face. Now I know in part; then I shall know fully, even as I am fully known.*

1 CORINTHIANS 13:12

## We See Dimly

One young man, who was academically in the top five percent of the nation, had a dream to become an engineer. However, when he applied to do graduate studies at the best engineering schools in the nation, he was turned down again and again while others with lower grades and scores were accepted. He couldn't understand it.

While he was waiting, he went on a mission trip with a group of doctors from his church. When he saw the doctors taking care of the people, something new was birthed on the inside. He thought, "I don't want to be an engineer. This is what I want to do with my life." After he returned home, he applied to medical school and was immediately accepted. God closed the doors to the engineering school on purpose, to push him into his divine destiny.

## Surrender Your Desires

*Return to your fortress, you prisoners of hope;*
*even now I announce that I will restore twice as much to you.*

ZECHARIAH 9:12

You may be discouraged because your plans have not worked out, but those closed doors were not an accident. That was God directing your steps. The reason God closed them is because He has something better in store. Will you trust Him? It may not make sense now, but one day it will. Remember, you're not really trusting Him if you are happy only when things go your way. Put your desires on the altar. "God, this is what I want, but let Your will, not mine, be done."

If you adopt this perspective and thank God for your closed doors just as much as for your open doors, you'll pass the test. I believe and declare you will see the exceeding, abundant, above-and-beyond future that God has in store.

## He Rules

*See, the Sovereign LORD comes with power,
and he rules with a mighty arm. See, his reward is with him,
and his recompense accompanies him.*

ISAIAH 40:10

Most of the time we believe God is in control when everything is going our way. We're getting good breaks. Business is up. The family is happy. We know God is directing our steps. Life is good. But having faith doesn't exempt us from difficulties. The storms of life come to every person. We get a bad medical report. A friend betrays us. Business takes a downturn. In the difficult times it's easy to think, "God, where are You?"

But the same God who is in control in the good times is just as in control in the tough times. God will not allow a storm unless He has a divine purpose for it. He never said He would prevent every difficulty, but God did promise He would use every difficulty.

## From Point A to B

*But Joseph said to them, "Don't be afraid. Am I in the place of God? You intended to harm me, but God intended it for good to accomplish what is now being done, the saving of many lives."*

GENESIS 50:19–20

Here's the key when you face difficult times: God will direct the winds of the storm to blow you where He wants you to go. We see storms as being negative, but God uses the storm to move you from point A to point B. The winds may be strong, the circumstances may look bad, but if you will stay in faith, not get bitter, not start complaining, those winds will blow you to a new level of your destiny.

It may have been meant for your harm, but God knows how to shift the winds. Instead of blowing you backward, He can cause them to blow you forward where you will come out better, stronger—and that storm also will move you to a place of greater blessing and greater influence.

*And God is faithful; he will not let you be tempted beyond what you can bear. But when you are tempted, he will also provide a way out so that you can endure it.*

1 CORINTHIANS 10:13

## God Is in Control

A lot of people say they have faith, but in the tough times they fall apart. They feel like God has disappointed them. But you have to remind yourself God is in control of that storm. Nothing happens without God's permission. If that storm was keeping you from your destiny, God would have never allowed it. If that person who left you, or that financial difficulty, or that legal situation was stopping God's plan for your life, He would have never permitted it.

The reason He did allow it was to move you one step closer to your divine destiny. Instead of using your faith to try to pray away every difficulty, you should use your faith to believe that when the winds stop blowing, you will be exactly where God wants you to be.

# A Never-ending Storm

*"Last night an angel of the God to whom I belong and whom I serve stood beside me and said, 'Do not be afraid, Paul. You must stand trial before Caesar; and God has graciously given you the lives of all who sail with you.'"*

ACTS 27:23–24

OCTOBER

2

God promised the Apostle Paul that he would stand before Caesar, yet on the way to Rome his ship was caught in a storm so strong and huge that the crew was certain they would all perish (Acts 27). Paul was doing the right thing, but was caught in what seemed to be a never-ending storm. Even so, he remained calm, believing God would not have allowed this storm if it would keep him from his destiny.

What happened? God used the winds of that storm to blow Paul to the small island of Malta where the father of the tribal chief was extremely sick. Paul prayed for him and he was healed. They brought others one by one to Paul. He prayed and God healed. The people of Malta never would have heard the Good News.

## Relinquish Control

*"Our God, will you not judge them? For we have no power to face this vast army that is attacking us. We do not know what to do, but our eyes are on you."*

2 CHRONICLES 20:12

Sometimes you face difficulties not because you're doing something wrong, but because you're doing something right. It's just another step on the way to your divine destiny. With most storms, we can see the end. But there are some storms that never seem like they'll end. You may have problems like that. It seems like they will never be resolved. You may think that in the natural you'll never get well or never get out of debt.

There comes a point when you've done everything you can. You've prayed. You've believed. Now you've got to quit fighting it. Quit trying to make it happen your way. Quit trying to force it to work out and just relinquish control. Let the storm take you where God wants you to go. God will never take you someplace where He won't sustain you.

## His Kingdom

*The LORD has established his throne in heaven, and his kingdom rules over all.*

PSALM 103:19

When my father died, it came as one of those storms we could not see the end of. Critics were saying Lakewood would never make it without my dad. But we had prayed and believed for healing. Our prayers weren't answered the way we wanted, on our timetable.

My father and I were best friends. All of the sudden he was gone. I had to do what I'm asking you to do. I said, "God, I know this storm is not a surprise to You. I'm turning loose of the sails, and I'm letting Your wind blow me to where You want me to go." That storm blew me from behind the scenes at Lakewood to the position I'm in now as leader of our church. I never dreamed I could speak in front of people, but God knew better.

*When a man's ways please the
LORD, He makes even his enemies
to be at peace with him.*

PROVERBS 16:7 NKJV

## Shifting
## the Winds

Stormy winds may be blowing in your life today. Maybe you can't see the end. Why don't you take a step of faith and say, "God, I'm letting You do it Your way. This storm cannot take me where You will not permit it to go."

When you do that, those winds will blow you to a new level of your destiny. It may not happen overnight, but God is faithful. His plan for your life will not be stopped by a storm, by a bad break, by the loss of a loved one, or by an injustice. God said no weapon formed against you will prosper. The battle is the Lord's. God is saying, "If you'll trust Me, I will shift those winds, and instead of blowing you backward, they will thrust you forward."

## Starting Over

*After Job had prayed for his friends, the L*ORD* restored his fortunes and gave him twice as much as he had before.*

JOB 42:10

OCTOBER
6

I read about a senior executive who had practically built a large home improvement company from the ground up. Then the company did a corporate restructuring, and its leaders decided that they didn't need him anymore. After thirty years, he had to start all over. He felt betrayed, but he understood this principle: God can direct the winds of the storm. Instead of becoming bitter and sitting around all angry, he forgave those who hurt him.

He let go of the job that didn't work out. He began to dream of new opportunities. He found some friends, and they started another company. This new company took off, and it has become one of the largest, most successful home improvement stores in all the nation. In fact, his new company put his old company out of business.

*Then the LORD spoke
to Job out of the storm.*

JOB 38:1

God knows how to shift the winds that were meant to destroy you and instead use them to increase you. Let go of whatever didn't work out. Forgive those who hurt you. When you dare say, "God, I trust You to make my wrongs right," then those winds trying to hold you back will shift direction and push you forward.

God is in complete control. If God wanted you to have that job from which you were laid off, you would still have it. If God wanted that person who left you to stay, that person would have stayed. If your prayers are not answered the way you wanted and on your timetable, don't be bitter. Don't be discouraged. Let it go. God has something better, something greater, something bigger in your future.

## Sustaining Faith

*"If we are thrown into the blazing furnace, the God we serve is able to deliver us from it . . . But even if he does not, we want you to know, Your Majesty, that we will not serve your gods or worship the image of gold you have set up."*

DANIEL 3:17–18

Shadrach, Meshach, and Abednego were about to be thrown into a fiery furnace because they wouldn't bow down before the king's golden idol (Daniel 3). I'm sure they prayed for deliverance. Sometimes God will deliver you from the fire. Other times God will make you fireproof and take you through the fire.

There are two kinds of faith. Delivering faith is when God keeps you from the fire, out of the adversity. But most of the time we need sustaining faith. Sustaining faith is when God takes you through the storm, through the difficulty, and the wind is blowing. You are filled with doubt, anxiety, fear, and bitterness. You have all these opportunities to get discouraged. But when you know that God is in control of the storm, you won't be worried. He will make you fireproof.

## Fireproof

*They saw that the fire had not harmed their bodies, nor was a hair of their heads singed; their robes were not scorched, and there was no smell of fire on them.*

DANIEL 3:27

After Shadrach, Meshach, and Abednego were thrown into the fiery furnace, the only thing the fire burned off were the cords that were holding them back. The God we serve knows how to burn up the limitations that are holding us back while not harming anything we need.

The same God who kept them safe in the fiery furnace has put a hedge of protection around you. Whether you realize it or not, you are fireproof. Don't complain about the storms. Don't be discouraged and think, "Oh, this is too big. This health issue, this financial difficulty, this legal battle, it will be the end of me." No, all it will to do is burn up the limitations that are holding you back. You are coming out stronger, increased, promoted, and without smelling like smoke, just like those teens.

### Show His Power

> *"And I will harden Pharaoh's heart, and he will pursue them. But I will gain glory for myself through Pharaoh and all his army, and the Egyptians will know that I am the* Lord.*"*

EXODUS 14:4

When Moses told Pharaoh, "God said, 'Let the people go,'" Pharaoh said no—not once, not twice, not three times. He said no again and again and again. What's interesting is the Scripture says, "God caused Pharaoh to say no." It wasn't even Pharaoh's choice. God caused him to refuse. Why? So God could show His power in a greater way.

Sometimes God will not remove the obstacle. He won't deliver you from the storm, not because He is mean, and not because He is trying to make your life miserable. He wants to show His favor in your life in a greater way. You may be in a storm, but remember: God is in control. Stay in peace.

*Daniel answered, "May the king live forever! My God sent his angel, and he shut the mouths of the lions. They have not hurt me, because I was found innocent in his sight."*

DANIEL 6:21–22

## In the Lions' Den

Daniel's enemies had him thrown into the lions' den, with hungry lions. When the king came to check on him, fully expecting to find him torn apart, he found Daniel sound asleep right next to hungry lions. He wasn't worried or hiding in the corner. Daniel was in peace. He knew he was lion proof. He knew the storm could not take him where God could not keep him.

Maybe you feel like you're in the lions' den. You could easily live all stressed out and worried. God is saying, "Come back to that place of peace." He has you in the palm of His hand. As long as you're being your best, honoring Him, He will shift the winds in your direction. Instead of defeating you, they will promote you. What is now your test will become your testimony.

## Help Others Overcome

*And Elisha prayed, "Open his eyes, LORD, so that he may see." Then the LORD opened the servant's eyes, and he looked and saw the hills full of horses and chariots of fire all around Elisha.*

2 KINGS 6:17

# OCTOBER 12

This lady I know found out she has cancer. She understands that God is in control of the storm. Her attitude was, "God, I've prayed. I've believed. Now I'm trusting You to take me where You want me to go." For one year she took chemotherapy and has been cancer free for more than six years. She is one of Lakewood's Prayer Partners, and she goes back to that hospital and volunteers, encouraging others facing cancer.

When God takes you through the fire, stay in faith, and you will see God's favor in a new way. I love the fact that this woman who survived cancer is now helping people overcome in that same area. Your test will become your testimony where you can tell people, "Hey, look. God did it for me. He can do it for you."

## Reach Out to Others

*Therefore confess your sins to each other and pray for each other so that you may be healed.*

JAMES 5:16

The storms you experience may be meant for your harm, but God knows how to direct the winds. He will not only protect you but also take you to a place where you can be a blessing to others in need. On the way out of your storm, don't be surprised if you have interruptions, inconveniences, and other setbacks you hadn't planned on. God ordained them so you can be a blessing.

Don't just look for your miracle. Become somebody's miracle. When you reach out to others in need—when you lift the fallen, when you encourage those who are down, when you befriend the lonely—your own breakthrough will come. One of the tests you have to pass is being good to others in the midst of your storm. They were meant to lift you to a higher level of your destiny.

## Be an Eagle

*"You yourselves have seen what I did to Egypt, and how I carried you on eagles' wings and brought you to myself."*

EXODUS 19:4

When an eagle faces a storm, he doesn't try to fight his way through the wind and the rain. He simply stretches out his wings, and he lets the strong winds lift him higher and higher. Finally, he rises above the storm, where it's as calm and peaceful as can be.

Maybe you are worried about a medical report, a child, or a challenge at work, and you can't sleep at night because of anxiety and fear. When the winds are blowing against you, it's easy to get frustrated and start fighting and trying to change what you were never meant to change. Be an eagle instead. Put your trust in God. "I've done everything I can. Now I'm going to quit struggling. I'm not trying to make it happen my way. God, I'm trusting You."

*"When you walk through the fire, you will not be burned; the flames will not set you ablaze."*

ISAIAH 43:2

## Promoted, Increased, Better

When you get to that place of peace, knowing that God is in control of the storm, then those winds meant to push you down will end up lifting you higher and higher. You may be in a difficulty right now. God didn't deliver you from the fire as He did the Hebrew teenagers. But let me encourage you. God has made you fireproof. You will come out of that fire promoted, increased, and better, without the smell of smoke.

What is your test now will soon become your testimony. Shake off the discouragement. Shake off the self-pity and get ready for God to do something new. Those winds blowing against you are about to shift direction. They will thrust you forward into the fullness of your destiny.

## Breaking Out

*But he drew back his hand, and behold, his brother was born first. And she said, What a breaking forth you have made for yourself!*

GENESIS 38:29 AMP

In Genesis 38, as a woman who is pregnant with twins gives birth, one of the baby's arms came out first. The midwife tied a small cord around it, planning to gently pull him, but before she could do that, the baby pulled his arm back and his brother broke through and was born first. One stretched and one settled.

In a similar way, inside each of us there are two people. One says, "I will become everything God has created me to be. I can do all things through Christ. I'm surrounded by God's favor." The other says, "I'll just have to learn to live with the way things are." One wants to stretch. The other wants to settle. You can choose which person you will be. Too many people make the choice to settle.

## Created to Excel

*"Tear down your father's altar to Baal and cut down the Asherah pole beside it. Then build a proper kind of altar to the Lord your God on the top of this height."*

JUDGES 6:25–26

Don't make the mistake of settling for "good enough." Good enough is not your destiny. You are a child of the Most High God. You have seeds of greatness on the inside. If you are to see the fullness of what God has in store, you have to have the right attitude: "I was created to excel, to live a healthy life, to overcome obstacles, to fulfill my destiny. I'm letting go of the things that didn't work out and reaching forward to the new things God has in store."

Perhaps you've become comfortable with good enough. But God is saying it's time to move forward. He has new levels in front of you, new opportunities, relationships, promotions, and breakthroughs. But you need to stir up what God put on the inside, stir up the dreams and the promises you've pushed down.

## Start Believing Again

*"I will lead the blind by ways they have not known, along unfamiliar paths I will guide them; I will turn the darkness into light before them and make the rough places smooth."*

ISAIAH 42:16

You may have come to the point where you feel your dreams are not going to happen. But God has it all figured out. If you start believing again, start dreaming again, start pursuing what God put in your heart, God will make a way where you can't see a way. He will connect you to the right people. He will open doors no man can shut. What God spoke over your life, what He promised you in the night, what He whispered in your spirit, those hidden dreams, He will bring to pass.

The good news is just because you gave up a dream doesn't mean God gave up. You may have changed your mind, but God didn't change His mind. He still has a victorious plan in front of you. Why don't you get in agreement with Him?

> *Some trust in chariots and some in horses, but we trust in the name of the LORD our God. They are brought to their knees and fall, but we rise up and stand firm.*
>
> PSALM 20:7–8

## Rise Up

I read about a star high school football player who dreamed of playing professional football. He came from a small town where all the children looked up to him as a hero. But he was considered too small to play in college, and he ended up taking a job at a pizza restaurant and going to junior college. One night he was delivering a pizza and a young boy answered the door and was starstruck. After a second or two, he said innocently, "What are *you* doing delivering pizzas?"

Those words lit a new fire on the inside for the young man. He started training hard and became bigger, stronger, quicker, and faster. He ended up playing for a major university and eventually was drafted in the first round to play professional football. Today, he is a star in the NFL, living out his dream.

## You Have So Much

*Terah took his son Abram . . .
and together they set out from
Ur of the Chaldeans to go to
Canaan. But when they came to
Harran, they settled there.*

GENESIS 11:31

# OCTOBER
# 20

My questions for you are: Have you settled somewhere way beneath what you know God has put in you? Have you given up on a dream, or let go of a promise, because it didn't happen the first time? Maybe you had a setback. Maybe somebody told you, "You're not talented enough. You're too old." But I ask you respectfully, "What are you doing there? You have so much in you. You are full of talent, ideas, creativity, and potential."

When God breathed His life into you, He put a part of Himself in you. You have the DNA of Almighty God. You were never created to be average, to barely get by, to always struggle, or to just have to take the leftovers. You were created as the head and not the tail.

## Stand Strong

*Therefore put on the full armor of God, so that when the day of evil comes, you may be able to stand your ground, and after you have done everything, to stand.*

EPHESIANS 6:13

You are equipped. Empowered. Fully loaded. Lacking nothing. Don't you dare settle for second best. Don't get stuck in a rut thinking that you've reached your limits. Draw the line in the sand and say, "That's it. I've let good enough be good enough long enough. Today is a new day. My dream may not have happened the first time I tried for it, or even the fifth time or the thirtieth time, but I'm not settling. I'm stretching my faith, looking for opportunities, taking steps to improve. I'm going to become everything God has created me to be."

When you do the natural, God will do the supernatural. When you do what you can, God will come and do what you cannot. Don't take the easy way out. Stand strong and fight the good fight of faith.

## Be a Warrior

*. . . the people of Judah were victorious because they relied on the LORD, the God of their ancestors.*

2 CHRONICLES 13:18

I want to light a new fire in you today. You have been armed with strength for every battle. That obstacle is no match for you. You have the most powerful force in the universe breathing in your direction. Be a warrior. Your marriage, your health, your dreams, and your children are worth fighting for. God didn't bring you this far to leave you here. Do not settle. Make it all the way in to your Promised Land.

If you're to be victorious, you must have a made-up mind. Be determined. You can't give up when life becomes difficult. You can't complain because it's taking a long time. You can't be discouraged because you went through a setback. Everything God promised you is worth fighting for, so you need to be in it for the long haul.

*Do not conform to the pattern of this world, but be transformed by the renewing of your mind. Then you will be able to test and approve what God's will is—his good, pleasing and perfect will.*

ROMANS 12:2

## Change Your Thinking

You may have hit a temporary delay to your dreams coming to pass, but that's okay. That won't stop you from fulfilling your destiny. Today can be your new beginning. God is breathing new life into your spirit. He has greater victories in front of you. Get a vision for it.

The first place we lose the battle is in our thinking. If you don't think you can be successful, you never will be. If you don't think you can overcome the past, or meet the right person, or accomplish your dreams, you'll be stuck right where you are. You have to change your thinking. The Creator of the universe is arranging things in your favor. He said no good thing would He withhold because you walk uprightly. He will not withhold the right person, the wisdom, the breaks, or the turnaround.

## Go for the Best

*Set your minds and keep*
*them set on what is above*
*(the higher things), not on the*
*things that are on the earth.*

COLOSSIANS 3:2 AMP

OCTOBER

# 24

God has a best, but you'll never see it if you keep taking the average. Yes, average is easier. You don't have to stretch. You don't have to leave your comfort zone. But you'll never be truly fulfilled if you keep settling for average. The good news is God already has the best in your future. He has the right person, a happy marriage, a successful career, health, wholeness, freedom, and victory.

Don't take the easy way out. The bests are worth fighting for. I can't think of much that would be sadder than to come to the end of life and have to wonder, "What could I have become if I didn't settle for good enough?" Make a decision with me that from now on you're only going for the best.

# The Enemy of Great

*Do you see a man who excels in his work? He will stand before kings; he will not stand before unknown men.*

PROVERBS 22:29 NKJV

If you're not seeing the things in your life that God promised in your spirit, keep moving forward. It's only temporary. Keep being your best, but see that as only temporary. You are just passing through. Don't settle there. If the medical report doesn't agree with what God says about you, don't accept it as the way it will always be.

Maybe God has blessed you with a great family, a wonderful job, and good health. You've seen His favor. But you know there are greater levels in front of you. It's easy to think, "I'm happy. I have no complaints. God has been good to me." But I've learned that good is the enemy of great. Don't let that be an excuse to keep you from God's best. Stir up your greatness. Stretch into a new level.

## Too Easily Satisfied

*"Why spend money on what is not bread, and your labor on what does not satisfy? Listen, listen to me, and eat what is good, and you will delight in the richest of fare."*

ISAIAH 55:2

God brought the people of Israel out of slavery to the Promised Land, a land flowing with milk and honey, a magnificent land so beautiful, luscious, green. That was the vision God had in front of them. All the people of Israel had to do was fight for the land. God had promised them the victory, but they were not willing to fight.

In the wilderness they had seen God's goodness part the Red Sea, bring water out of a rock, and rain down manna from Heaven. But that was all only temporary provision. I believe one reason they settled there so easily is because they had seen God's provisions in the wilderness. They were too easily satisfied. They didn't realize everything God had done up to that point was only to sustain them until they reached their land of abundance.

## The Land of Abundance

*When the LORD your God brings you into the land he swore to your fathers, to Abraham, Isaac and Jacob, to give you— a land with large, flourishing cities you did not build . . .*

DEUTERONOMY 6:10

Don't make the mistake made by the people of Israel when they built houses in the wilderness where they should have pitched tents. Thank God for His goodness, protection, provision, and favor. But don't let your temporary provision become permanent. If it's not what God put in your spirit, be bold enough to say, "God, this is all great. You've been awesome in my life, and I thank You for it. But I believe this is only temporary provision. Where You're taking me is to a land of abundance, a place like I've never experienced before."

Yes, God has been good to you, but you haven't seen anything yet. What God has in your future will supersede what you've seen in the past. That's not being selfish. That's releasing your faith for the fullness of your destiny.

## Out of the Ordinary

*"May the LORD, the God of your ancestors, increase you a thousand times and bless you as he has promised!"*

DEUTERONOMY 1:11

L et those words sink down into your spirit. I don't know about you, but I can't settle here. I've got to pull up my stakes. God has a thousand times more: more joy, more peace, more influence, more wisdom, more ideas, more creativity, and more good breaks. Take the limits off God.

When Joshua was leading the people of Israel, God said, "Joshua, you have not passed this way before." God is saying the same thing to us. Something out of the ordinary is coming your way; new levels of favor, unprecedented opportunities, or divine connections. People are already lined up to be good to you. You don't have to find them. They'll come find you. When you honor God, His blessings will chase you down. You won't be able to outrun the good things of God.

*. . . stir up (rekindle the embers of, fan the flame of, and keep burning) the [gracious] gift of God, [the inner fire] that is in you . . .*

2 TIMOTHY 1:6 AMP

## All the Way

My challenge to you is this: Don't settle where you are in your health, your relationships, your career, or your walk with the Lord. Keep stretching. Keep growing. Keep believing. Keep dreaming. Don't let good enough be good enough. Be determined to become everything God created you to be. It's time to pull up your stakes. Pack up your belongings. Start moving forward. Enlarge your vision. Make room in your thinking for the new thing God wants to do. Don't let your temporary provision become permanent.

If you'll learn this principle of stretching and not settling, you will see the fullness of what God has in store. I believe you will overcome obstacles and accomplish dreams. As Joshua did, you're going to make it all the way to your Promised Land.

## Seeds of Increase

*I praise you because I am*
*fearfully and wonderfully made;*
*your works are wonderful,*
*I know that full well.*

PSALM 139:14

OCTOBER
# 30

When God created us, He put seeds of increase on the inside. We were never made to reach one level and stop. We were created to grow, to move forward, and to increase. We should be constantly breaking the barriers of the past, taking new ground for our families, and advancing God's Kingdom. But throughout life there will always be forces trying to contain us, to keep us in a box and to limit our influence.

Here's the good news. You are uncontainable. The forces in you are greater than the forces trying to contain you. If you're to become everything God has created you to be, you can't get stuck in a rut and think you've reached your limits. Keep stretching your faith, looking for new opportunities, new ideas, and new ways to expand your influence.

## You Have an Anointing

### OCTOBER

# 31

*But you have an anointing*
*from the Holy One, and all*
*of you know the truth.*

1 JOHN 2:20

When I was twelve years old, I played football. The running back on an opposing team was very fast and almost impossible to stop. Our coach came up with a special defense to try and contain him. But the coach could have put the whole team on him and he still would have run by us all. Even when we were able to grab him, it was like he was covered with oil. He was uncontainable.

That's the way I want you to see yourself. You have the Spirit of the Living God on the inside. His anointing on your life is just like oil. When something tries to stop you or hold you down, it doesn't have a chance. In your imagination you just twist and turn and see that something slide off. You are uncontainable.

## A Barrier Breaker

*"Let us acknowledge the LORD; let us press on to acknowledge him. As surely as the sun rises, he will appear; he will come to us like the winter rains, like the spring rains that water the earth."*

HOSEA 6:3

I'm here to infect you with a God virus. It says, "You were made for more, to influence more, to accomplish more, to love more, to give more, and to have more." God is saying you have not touched the surface of what He has in store for you. He will take you places you've never dreamed of. He will bring opportunities that give you amazing influence. Your best days are still out in front of you.

You need to dig your heels in and say, "I will not be contained by negative people, by the way I was raised, by mistakes I've made, by injustice, disappointment, or even some handicap. I have my mind made up. Where I am is not where I'm staying. I'm rising higher. I'm a barrier breaker. I'm taking new ground for God's Kingdom."

*After they prayed, the place where they were meeting was shaken. And they were all filled with the Holy Spirit and spoke the word of God boldly.*

ACTS 4:31

## Uncon- tainable

I love the story in Acts 4, in which Peter and John prayed for people and they became well. Great miracles had taken place. They had a big service. All kinds of good things happened. But instead of being happy about it, the city leaders opposed them and ordered it to stop. They were saying in effect, "We're pushing them down to lessen their influence and contain them."

But Peter and John understood this principle. They knew: "We cannot be contained. God put this dream in our hearts, and as long as we stay in faith, nothing can shut it down." Their message was not restricted. It spread like wildfire, and we're still talking about it today. In the same way, you cannot be contained. If you'll just keep pressing forward, God will open doors that no man can shut.

## Increase Your Influence

*For I command you today to love the LORD your God, to walk in obedience to him . . . then you will live and increase, and the LORD your God will bless you in the land you are entering to possess.*

DEUTERONOMY 30:16

Nelson Mandela was put in prison because he opposed the government of apartheid in South Africa. He could have thought, "I did my best, gave it my all. I guess it wasn't meant to be." Instead, Mr. Mandela knew he couldn't be contained by people, by injustice, by racism, by hatred, or even by prison walls. Twenty-seven years later, he walked out a free man. Eventually, he became president of that same country and won the Nobel Peace Prize.

What God has destined for your life will come to fulfillment. God is going to increase your influence. Rid yourself of that limited mentality and press forward in faith. God will make you a barrier breaker. God is about to thrust you into a new level of your destiny. You cannot be contained.

## Power of His Word

*". . . so is my word that goes out from my mouth:*
*It will not return to me empty, but will accomplish what*
*I desire and achieve the purpose for which I sent it."*

**ISAIAH 55:11**

When the Apostle Paul was imprisoned for spreading the Good News, his captors thought they were containing him. Paul could have become depressed, discouraged, and given up. Instead, his attitude was, "I may not be able to go out and minister, but I do have a pen and paper. I can write." Paul wrote much of the New Testament from a prison cell. His captors thought they were containing him, but their plan backfired. Paul had more influence with his writings than he ever had in person.

God is going to increase your influence. The Scripture says God will cause His face to shine down on us. That's His favor. You need to start expecting this favor as never before. God wants you to be a barrier breaker. He wants you to take new ground for the Kingdom.

## A Child of God

*See what great love the Father has lavished on us, that we should be called children of God! And that is what we are!*

1 JOHN 3:1

My father grew up extremely poor. He developed a barely-get-by mentality. He certainly never thought he would have any influence. It took him years and years to get rid of a poverty mind-set, a second-class mentality. But one day he realized he didn't have to be contained by how he was raised and that he was created to live an abundant life. He developed this new mind-set as a child of the Most High God.

My father was a barrier breaker. He believed he could rise higher. He was not contained by how he was raised and what was modeled growing up. He saw God do amazing things in his life. Refuse to see yourself as second class, poor and defeated. Don't be content to just scrape by with no influence, no respect, and no credibility.

*But by the grace of God I am
what I am, and His grace
toward me was not in vain.*

1 CORINTHIANS 15:10 NKJV

## Taking New Ground

Thank God, this is a new day. There's a new generation rising up with people who say, "I know who I am: a child of Almighty God. I don't have to be contained by how I was raised, by what I've seen in the past. I know I am a barrier breaker. I am a person of influence. So I'm moving forward and taking new ground, not just for my family but also to advance God's Kingdom."

It all begins in your thinking. You need to see yourself differently. You are a barrier breaker. You are uncontainable. You have so much talent in you, so much potential. There are seeds of greatness on the inside. If you will break free from your limited mind-set and enlarge your vision, you will see God take you places that you've never even dreamed of.

## Greater Influence

*Every day they continued to meet together . . . praising God and enjoying the favor of all the people. And the Lord added to their number daily those who were being saved.*

ACTS 2:46–47

# 7

Our former church campus was on a very small side street in a rural section of town. I tried to go the traditional route and buy some property and build a sanctuary on it for Lakewood Church. But God's dream for our lives is always so much bigger than our own.

God gave us a premier building in the fourth largest city in America. Today, we're not on a side street. We're on the second busiest freeway in the nation, sitting on a prime piece of property. We broke barriers. God didn't just give us a building. He increased our influence. God helped us pave the way, to go further. Now other people can come behind us and do the same thing. That's the way God wants it to be. Every generation should increase.

## An Explosion

*"For the earth will be filled with the knowledge of the glory of the LORD as the waters cover the sea."*

HABAKKUK 2:14

When I was growing up, you could hear Christian music only in our church services. This is a new day. My children were watching an *American Idol* show, the number one program on television at the time, where all of the contestants sang a song that our friend Darlene Zschech wrote, "Shout to the Lord, all the earth, let us sing." God is increasing our influence. He is causing our gifts and talents to come out in greater ways.

Rid yourself of every limited thought. You have exactly what you need. You have gifts, talents, ideas, inventions, books, and movies. They are just waiting to come out. When they do, it will be like an explosion. You'd better get ready. God is about to thrust you into a new level of your destiny. You cannot be contained.

## For the King

> *"Very truly I tell you, whoever believes in me will do the works I have been doing, and they will do even greater things than these, because I am going to the Father."*
>
> JOHN 14:12

It's been said that the most famous sports facility in the world is Yankee Stadium. A while back, as the team owners were finishing building their new ballpark, they invited us to bring one of our "Nights of Hope" to New York City and become the first nonbaseball event held in the new Yankee Stadium. When my staff told me, I thought they were joking. They could invite the Rolling Stones or Madonna. But instead they invited this minister from Texas. What was God doing? He was increasing our influence. We were able to take new ground for the King.

God is not limited by your circumstances. God is not contained by your education, by your environment, or by how you were raised. All God has to do is breathe in your direction.

*Trust in the LORD and do good.*
*Then you will live safely in*
*the land and prosper.*

PSALM 37:3 NLT

## Make Your Mark

D r. Todd Price grew up very poor. But as a twelve-year-old, he was moved by a television program that said for $15 a month he could sponsor and feed a starving child. He started mowing lawns and used that money to sponsor a child. Forty years later, Dr. Price has a successful medical practice, and so far he has given more than $250 million in medicine to needy people around the world.

Dr. Price is a barrier breaker. In the natural, it didn't look like he could ever go to medical school or ever make much of his life. But he didn't allow those strongholds to take root. Deep down he knew he was uncontainable. He knew the Creator of the Universe was breathing in his direction. Today, Dr. Price is making a mark that cannot be erased.

## As You Are

*"Let it be to me according to your word."*

LUKE 1:38 NKJV

# NOVEMBER
## 11

I'm asking you to get rid of your excuses. Quit thinking, "I'm not talented enough. I've made too many mistakes. I've got this handicap." Let these words sink deep down into your spirit: You are uncontainable. You're a barrier breaker. God wants to use you just as you are. He wants to use you to influence others. Get a vision for it. You can set a new standard for your family. Unlock what's on the inside. Your seeds of greatness are waiting to take root and flourish.

And know this: God is breathing in your direction. Your vision is increasing. Your faith is rising. Your dreams are coming back to life. You have not seen your best days. What God has in store in your future will supersede anything you could even imagine.

## Advance
## His Kingdom

*"Lord, the God of our ancestors,
are you not the God who is in
heaven? You rule over all the
kingdoms of the nations. Power
and might are in your hand, and
no one can withstand you."*

2 CHRONICLES 20:6

Take the limitations off God and off yourself. Quit looking at what you don't have and what you can't do and how big your obstacles are. Shake that off and have the attitude: "I am uncontainable. I'm a child of the Most High God. I will fulfill my destiny. These people trying to push me down can't contain me. If God will be for me, who dares be against me?"

What you've seen God do in the past will pale in comparison to what God is about to do. I declare that you will go places you've never dreamed of. You will have influence in circles that you've never imagined. You will be a barrier breaker. You will take new ground for your family. You will advance God's Kingdom. Your gifts and talents will come out in a greater way.

# The Pearl

*"Again, the kingdom of heaven is like a
merchant looking for fine pearls."*

MATTHEW 13:45

You may not have realized this, but pearls—one of the most beautiful, natural, and expensive jewels—are formed from irritations. Oysters feed off the bottom of the ocean, and occasionally something will become lodged on the inside of the shell and irritate the oyster. It responds by covering it with the same material used to create the shell. When fully coated, the "irritant" becomes a beautiful pearl.

In the same way, God designed every irritation in our lives to become a pearl. He allows us to be in uncomfortable situations where we're not getting our way, not being treated right, or things are not happening as fast as we would like. This pressure brings to light impurities in our character, things like pride, selfishness, being critical, or easily offended. These are traits we need to get rid of.

## Faith and Patience

*We do not want you to become lazy, but to imitate those who through faith and patience inherit what has been promised.*

HEBREWS 6:12

Life irritations were designed to help you grow, to help you develop the pearl. I've learned you can't pray away every uncomfortable situation or trial. God allows difficulties to help us grow. He uses people who are hard to get along with like sandpaper to rub the rough edges off us. If we don't understand the process God uses, we'll go through life frustrated, wondering why God is not answering our prayers, and running from every difficulty.

Understand that the irritation is not God trying to make our lives miserable. It's just that God knows there is a pearl in each of us waiting to be formed. The only way we can develop them is by passing these tests, by being kind to an unpleasant coworker, biting our tongues at times, or by keeping a good attitude even when stuck in traffic.

## Beyond the Irritations

*To this you were called, because Christ suffered for you, leaving you an example, that you should follow in his steps.*

1 PETER 2:21

The Apostle Paul said in Romans 8:18, "Our present sufferings are not worth comparing with the glory that will be revealed in us." Paul was mistreated, lied about, persecuted, and had to put up with all kinds of unfairness, but he didn't complain or try to run from difficulties. He realized that to grow, you may have to suffer through irritations as God refines you.

Our attitude should be: "If this is where God has me, I must need it. I'm not fighting against it. I'm not trying to pray it away. I'm embracing the place where I am. I know God has given me the grace to be here. He has put me on the potter's wheel, so I'm keeping a good attitude because I know right beyond this irritation is a beautiful pearl."

*Now if we are children, then we are heirs—heirs of God and co-heirs with Christ, if indeed we share in his sufferings in order that we may also share in his glory.*

ROMANS 8:17

## Share His Glory

The Scripture says if we're to share in Christ's glory, we must be willing to share in His sufferings. This suffering doesn't mean accidents, tragedy, cancer, injustice, or abuse. The suffering the Scripture refers to occurs when we have to say no to our flesh, when we remain calm after we don't get our way, and when we stay in faith even when life seems unfair. When we pass those tests, our flesh—the human or natural part of us—will not like it. We will be uncomfortable. We will want to do what we feel like doing. But if we stay on the high road and suffer through the discomfort, it allows God to refine us. Our character is being developed in this way. Our pearls are being polished.

## We Are the Clay

*Yet you, Lord, are our*
*Father. We are the clay,*
*you are the potter; we are*
*all the work of your hand.*

ISAIAH 64:8

NOVEMBER

# 17

We all start off at the same place. We're lumps of hard clay. We have impurities, including pride, selfishness, impatience, anger, and resentment. God puts us on the potter's wheel and begins to spin us around. When He comes across one of those lumps, those impurities, He will put us in a situation to work it out. The key is to pass the test.

Don't fight against everything you don't like. Learn to overlook an offense. Make allowances for somebody who is hard to get along with. Quit feeling hurt because someone offended you. Toughen up and pass those tests. If we let God refine us so we treat people well and handle disappointments without complaining, we can be used for God's highest purposes.

*"See, I have refined you, though
not as silver; I have tested you in
the furnace of affliction."*

ISAIAH 48:10

The Scripture talks about the "furnace of affliction," where you could either give up and get sour or you can say, "God, I'll show You what I'm made of. I'll forgive those who hurt me. I'll keep believing even though it looks impossible. I'll stay in faith even though it was unfair." When you pass those tests, something is deposited on the inside that nothing can take away. There is a trust, a confidence, a knowing that can be developed only by going through the fire of affliction. I've learned that God is not as interested in changing my circumstances as He is in changing me.

Where you are is not nearly as important as who you are. While God is changing the "where," allow Him to change the "who." He wants to bring the pearl out of you.

## Bear Much Fruit

*"This is to my Father's glory, that you bear much fruit, showing yourselves to be my disciples."*

JOHN 15:8

We should be growing, bearing more fruit in our lives. If you are still getting upset over the same things that upset you a year ago, it's time to grow up. If the same person who was getting on your nerves five years ago is still stealing your joy, you need to look inside and make some changes. God may not change them. He wants to use them to change you.

We cannot waste time going around the same mountain year after year like the people of Israel headed toward the Promised Land. Put your foot down and say, "That's it. This is a new day. I will not keep having a bad attitude every time I don't get my way, arguing with my spouse over the same petty issues, giving in to the same temptation time and time again."

*Know then in your heart that as a man disciplines his son, so the LORD your God disciplines you.*

DEUTERONOMY 8:5

## On the Potter's Wheel

The sooner you make the necessary changes in your life and pass the irritation tests, the better off you will be. There is a pearl in you. You may have a lot of rough edges, but know that as long as you are moving forward, God is pleased with you. But if your attitude doesn't change, God will keep you on the potter's wheel. You can pray all day long, "God, deliver me from these rude people. God, take away all these inconveniences. God, change my spouse." It's not going to happen. God wants you to change.

The truth is, God may never remove the irritation, but you will grow to such a point that it won't even bother you anymore. What's happening? Your character is being developed. Your pearl is being polished.

## Test of Quality

*Dear friends, do not be surprised at the fiery
ordeal that has come on you to test you, as though
something strange were happening to you.*

1 PETER 4:12

Trials are to test our quality. We may not like
it, but trials bring to light things we need to
deal with. Most of the time you are tested in areas
where you need to improve. For instance, if you
struggle with being impatient, don't be surprised
if you get behind every slow driver out there and
catch every red light.

God has you there for one reason: to refine
you. You've got to recognize that trial, that irritation, is not a coincidence. It's a test of your quality. Are you getting upset and losing your cool
as you've done in the past? Or are you saying,
"I recognize this is an opportunity to grow. God
wouldn't have me here if I didn't need it, so I'm
staying in peace, keeping a good attitude, and
passing this test."

## Change Me

*When Peter saw [John], he asked, "Lord, what about him?" Jesus answered, ". . . what is that to you? You must follow me."*

JOHN 21:20–22

Early in our marriage, I would ask Victoria if she was ready to leave. She would say yes, so I would go sit in the car and wait and wait and wait. I'd go back in all frustrated and say, "You said you were ready." "I am ready," she'd say. This happened time and time again. I would get so stressed. I was praying, "God, You've got to change her into this or that."

I had her on the potter's wheel. One day I realized I'm not the potter; God is. It's funny, God never changed her. He used her to change me. My prayers backfired. God has a sense of humor. So often we pray for God to change the other person. I've learned not to pray for God to change somebody else without first saying, "God, change me."

## Joy and Peace

> *". . . the joy of the LORD is your strength."*
>
> NEHEMIAH 8:10

A lady who attends Lakewood Church always comes without her husband. For years she came forward for prayer with a list of all the things she wanted God to fix. She didn't think she could be happy unless they all turned around. The main thing she wanted to change was her husband. Then, I saw her one day and she was beaming with joy and more at peace than I had ever seen her. I thought something must have worked out. But she said, "No, my husband is just the same, but I've changed. I don't let him keep me from enjoying my life."

What happened? She let that irritation become a pearl. When you can be happy, not because of your circumstances, but in spite of your circumstances, then something is deposited on the inside that nothing can take away.

> *"I know, my God, that*
> *you test the heart and are*
> *pleased with integrity."*

1 CHRONICLES 29:17

## The Creator's Smile

When I was in New York City, I went to a little diner to eat breakfast. A gentleman came up and said that when he'd walked into the restaurant, the person in front of him let the door slam in his face purposefully. Normally this gentleman might have told him off, but he said he'd recently watched my sermon on the potter's wheel and could hear me saying, "Let it go, and God will fight your battles."

He let it go, and when he did, he felt a joy bubbling up on the inside like something he had never felt before. When I walked into the diner five minutes later, he said he nearly passed out. "I knew that was God saying He was pleased with me." When you pass these tests, the Creator of the universe is smiling down on you.

## He Will Purify

*He will sit as a refiner and
purifier of silver; he will
purify the Levites and refine
them like gold and silver.*

MALACHI 3:3

# NOVEMBER
# 25

God works in our lives by changing us little by
little, from glory to glory. But on the way to
the glory there may be a little bit of suffering that
we have to endure. There may be times we try to
get out of it, but God will smile and say, "Not yet."

God sees your value. He knows what He is
making you into. Sometimes when we look at
ourselves we think, "I've got a lot of flaws. I've got
a hot temper. I've got a problem with my mouth."
We see the clay, but God sees the beautiful vessel.
The good news is you're not a finished product.
God is still working on you, and if you will work
with God and let Him remove those impurities,
He will make more out of your life than you've
ever dreamed.

## All His Ways

*He is the Rock, his works are perfect, and all his ways are just. A faithful God who does no wrong, upright and just is he.*

DEUTERONOMY 32:4

Too many people go through life thinking somebody owes them something. If they didn't have a perfect childhood, they're angry at their parents. If they were laid off after many years with a company, they're upset with their bosses. Or maybe they came down with an illness. Life threw them a curve. Now, they have a chip on their shoulder and bitterness on the inside. They ask: "If God was so good, how could He let this happen to me?"

But God never promised life would be fair. He did promise that if you stay in faith, He would take what is meant for your harm and use it to your advantage. Nothing that happens to you is a surprise to God. It might not have been fair. But that didn't catch God off guard.

## Get Over It

*But the LORD replied, "Is it right for you to be angry?"*

JONAH 4:4

My message is very simple, and I offer it with respect: Get over whatever wrongs have been done to you. Don't think you were cheated and use it as an excuse to be bitter. If you get over it, God will still get you to where you're supposed to be. The person who did you wrong in a relationship, the betrayal, or the divorce might have caused you pain, but if you get over it, quit reliving all the hurt, and move forward, you'll come to the new beginning God has in store.

Don't let bitter feelings take root. God knows what He's doing. God wasn't having a bad day when He created you. You are not at a disadvantage. You have been fearfully and wonderfully made. Take the hand you've been dealt and make the most of it.

*For you created my inmost being; you knit me together in my mother's womb.*

PSALM 139:13

# Don't Compare

My mother had polio as a child and wore a brace on her leg because one of her legs is much smaller than the other. When she buys shoes, she has to buy two pairs of the same shoe because her feet are different sizes. That could have embarrassed her. She could have shrunk back and tried to hide it. But she never did. My mother knows she was made in the image of Almighty God.

Why? She got over it. She didn't make excuses. She didn't fall into the self-pity trap. Sometimes we may be tempted to think, "If I had a different life, I'd be better off. If I had his talent or her family or their house, things would be great." Don't compare your situation to anyone else's. You're not running their race.

# The Grace You Need

*Your eyes saw my unformed body; all the days ordained for me were written in your book before one of them came to be.*

PSALM 139:16

## NOVEMBER
# 29

I t may seem like others have more advantages or more going for them, but God has given you the grace you need to fulfill your destiny. You're not anointed to be them. You are anointed to be you. So shake off any self-pity and any bitterness. Your attitude should be: "Nobody owes me anything. I am not at a disadvantage. I didn't get left out, shortchanged, passed over, or cheated. I am equipped, empowered, and anointed. All the forces of darkness cannot keep me from my destiny."

I'm asking you to get over anything holding you back. Don't be pitiful when you can be powerful. The Creator of the universe breathed His life into you. Every day of your life already has been written in God's book. The good news is that your book ends in victory.

## Turn the Page

*Am I now trying to win the approval of human beings, or of God? Or am I trying to please people? If I were still trying to please people, I would not be a servant of Christ.*

GALATIANS 1:10

We all go through tough times, but we're not supposed to stay there. Keep turning the page and you'll come to another victory. God knew there'd be unfair situations in your life. That's why He's arranged a comeback for every setback, a vindication for every wrong, and a new beginning for every disappointment. Don't let one bad break, a divorce, or a rough childhood cause you to sour on life.

If your boss didn't give you the promotion, God has something better in store. If certain "friends" leave you out and won't give you their approval, you have Almighty God's approval, and that's all that matters. Maybe your business didn't make it. Don't condemn yourself. You are not a failure. You took a step of faith, and a door closed. That means you're one step closer to an open door.

## Fight the Good Fight

*I have fought the good fight,*
*I have finished the race, I have kept the faith.*

2 TIMOTHY 4:7

When you are knocked down, don't stay down. Get back up. Nothing good will happen as long as you're down on yourself, down on life, focused on your mistakes and your disadvantages. That attitude will keep you from the amazing future God has in store.

Fight the good fight of faith. God did not bring you this far to leave you. When the going gets tough, the tough have to get going. Get over the disappointment, self-pity, and doubt. You have been armed with strength for this battle. The enemy doesn't have the final say; God has the final say. So, keep turning that page, praying, believing, being your best, being good to other people, and you will come into another chapter, a chapter of victory.

## No Matter What

*"Though he slay me, yet will I hope in him . . ."*

JOB 13:15

Think about the story of Job. He had a lot to get over. He lost his health, his family, and his business. If anybody had a right to have a chip on his shoulder, to be angry and bitter, it was Job. He loved God. He was being his best. Yet his life was turned upside down. Job could have given up on life and blamed God. Instead, right in the middle of his challenges, he looked up to the heavens and said in effect, "No matter what comes my way, I'm not getting bitter, angry, offended, or carrying a chip on my shoulder. My situation may not be fair. But I know a secret. My God is still on the Throne. He will make my wrongs right. I'm going to get over it and keep moving forward."

**Double Up** | *The LORD blessed the latter part of Job's life more than the former part.*

JOB 42:12

After Job had endured his trials and prayed for his friends who had brought false accusations against him, he came out with twice what he had before. When you get over it, you position yourself for double. When you forgive someone who did you wrong, get ready for double. When you have a good attitude even though life has thrown you a curve, get ready for double. When you go through life being your best even though it seems like you're at a disadvantage, get ready for double.

Don't let what people say or tough circumstances pull you down. No matter what comes your way, you get over it and keep moving forward. When you do that, you better get ready. God says to you what He said to Job, "Double is coming your way."

> *"He causes his sun to rise on the evil and the good, and sends rain on the righteous and the unrighteous."*

MATTHEW 5:45

## Through the Storms

I'd love to tell you that if you have faith and you love God, then you'd never have any difficulties. But that's not reality. I can tell you when the storms come, if you know the Lord as your shepherd, you will not be defeated.

When it's all said and done, you may go through the fire, through the flood, and through the famine, but you'll come out standing strong. Don't be discouraged by the storm. Don't fall into self-pity. "I don't know what I did wrong." You may not have done anything wrong. Maybe it's because you're doing something right. You may be taking new ground for the Kingdom. The enemy will not roll out the red carpet to allow you to fulfill your destiny. But know this: The forces for you are greater than the forces against you.

## God's Child

*Although my father and my
mother have forsaken me,
yet the Lord will take me up
[adopt me as His child].*

PSALM 27:10 AMP

God is not surprised by what was lacking or hurtful in your past. Don't use those things as an excuse to go through life feeling short-changed. Move forward. This is a new day. God knew who your parents would be. He knew what kind of environment you would be raised in. I'm not making light of hardships and hurts. Some people grew up in very unfair and difficult situations. They didn't get the love, the approval, or the support they should have had. But if they start looking to God, He will make up for everything they lacked.

To feel sorry for yourself will keep you from the amazing future God has in store. If you have the right attitude, then instead of being a setback, it'll be a setup for God to do something great in your life.

## Don't Look Around

*And so we know and rely on the love God has for us. God is love. Whoever lives in love lives in God, and God in them.*

1 JOHN 4:16

Some people were never taught to show love, to express approval. They had no role models for that. They pass down what they've experienced. If you look only to other people, you'll be disappointed. They will let you down. And if you're not careful, you'll become bitter and resentful toward them. You may think, "You owe me." But maybe God is teaching you to rely not on people but on Him. Quit trying to make another person be everything to you. No one has 100 percent. No one can meet all your needs—it doesn't matter how good that person may be, how loving or how kind.

I've heard it said, "If you want someone to give you 100 percent, don't look around. Look up. God is the only One who can give you everything you need."

## No Bitter Root

*See to it that no one falls short of the grace of God and that no bitter root grows up to cause trouble and defile many.*

HEBREWS 12:15

I've learned that a bitter root will always produce bitter fruit. Bitter people don't have good relationships. They're too negative. When we're bitter, it affects our attitudes. We see everything through a critical lens. Nothing is ever good enough. Bitter people can smile on the outside, but on the inside they're critical. Bitterness infects everything you do and follows you everywhere you go.

When we hold on to things we should let go, refusing to forgive, remembering the worst, we only poison our own lives. God is saying, "Get over it." Life is flying by. You don't have time to waste another minute being negative, offended, or bitter. If someone did you wrong or you had a bad break, get over it and God will make it up to you. God is still on the Throne.

> *Jesus looked at them and said,*
> *"With man this is impossible,*
> *but not with God; all things*
> *are possible with God."*

MARK 10:27

# God Determines Destinies

My friend Nick Vujicic was born with no arms and no legs. He could be sitting around saying, "God, it's not fair. I have no reason to live. I have no future in front of me." No, Nick has taken the cards he was dealt and he's making the most of it. Today, he's a minister who travels the world challenging people not to let any disadvantage hold them back.

Everyone has challenges, but you can't "if only" your way through life. What happened to you may seem like a disadvantage in your eyes, but it is not a disadvantage in God's eyes. It's not keeping you from your destiny. It will *thrust* you into your destiny. Now you have to do your part and get over anything that's holding you back. No one else can determine your destiny. God does that.

## You Are Responsible

*Then the LORD said to Cain, "Why are you angry?*
*Why is your face downcast? If you do what is right,*
*will you not be accepted?"*

GENESIS 4:6–7

Are you making excuses for why you can't succeed or be happy? Get over it. You are responsible for your happiness. You need to forgive those who hurt you, not for their sakes but for your own. Forgive so you can be free. Nothing in life has happened to you. It's happened for you. Every disappointment. Every wrong. Even every closed door has helped make you into who you are. You are not defined by your past. You are prepared by your past. You may have encountered some great obstacles, but only because God has a great future in front of you. If you will get over what you think is a disadvantage, God will take what looks like a liability and turn it into an asset.

## Pull Up the Roots

*Get rid of all bitterness, rage, anger, harsh words,*
*and slander, as well as all types of evil behavior.*

EPHESIANS 4:31 NLT

Get over those things that haven't worked out as you'd hoped. Get over the mistakes you've made. Get over the disappointments. Something may have surprised you and set you back, but it's not a surprise to God. He's already arranged the comeback. Your attitude should be: "Nobody owes me anything. I am not going through life with a chip on my shoulder. I'm letting go of those things that didn't work out. I'm forgiving those who did me wrong. I'm pulling up the roots of bitterness, and I'm moving forward into the amazing future God has in store."

If you learn this simple principle to get over it, I believe and declare no disappointment, no bad break, no injustice, will keep you from your destiny. God will take what's meant for your harm and use it to your advantage.

## Faith He Can See

*When Jesus saw their faith, he said to the paralyzed man, "Son, your sins are forgiven."*

MARK 2:5

The Scripture tells us there was a paralyzed man who asked four of his friends to carry him to a home where Jesus was teaching. When they arrived it was so crowded they couldn't get in. I'm sure they were exhausted and could have easily given up, but instead they hoisted him up on the roof and began to take the roof tiles off. Finally, they lowered this paralyzed man into the room.

The Scripture says, "When Jesus saw their faith." God is looking for people who have faith that He can see—not just hear, not just believe, but a faith that is visible, a faith that is demonstrated. There were other people in the room who had the same opportunity but didn't get well. The difference was this man put actions behind his belief, and he received his healing.

*He gives strength to
the weary and increases
the power of the weak.*

ISAIAH 40:29

## Take One Step

One day I talked to a gentleman who'd smoked cigarettes for thirty years. He'd been smoking three packs a day for the last ten years. He wanted to quit. He tried, but nothing worked. He had prayed. He had believed. Then one day he heard you have to put actions behind your faith. So he started to break his nicotine habit by immediately throwing away three cigarettes whenever he'd open a new pack. After a couple months, he wasn't missing those three anymore, so he doubled up and began throwing out six from each pack. By slowly cutting back, he no longer smokes at all.

Here's my point: The power came when he took it one step further and showed God he meant business by putting action behind his faith.

## Small Steps

*"If you are willing and obedient, you will eat the good things of the land . . ."*

ISAIAH 1:19

# DECEMBER
# 13

Are you doing something to show God you're serious about your dreams coming to pass? God is not moved by our needs. He's concerned about our needs, but God is moved by our faith. The action you take does not have to be something big. It could be just a small step to show God your faith. When God sees you doing what you can to get well, when He sees you getting to work a little earlier because you want that promotion, when He sees you bypass the cookie jar because you've been believing to lose weight—that is when extraordinary things will happen.

When you take small steps to show your faith, you'll find that you have a power to do what you couldn't do before. You'll see favor and opportunity that will thrust you to a new level.

## Actions Speak Louder

*"Go and tell Hezekiah, 'This is what the LORD, the God of your father David, says: I have heard your prayer and seen your tears; I will add fifteen years to your life.'"*

ISAIAH 38:5

When my sister Lisa was about three years old, she wanted to go to the office with my father, and she wouldn't take no for an answer. She was so determined she ignored his "no" and got dressed as if she were going with him. When she realized he was about to leave, she came on a run, struggling to put her last shoe on. His heart melted. When he saw how badly she wanted to go and how determined she was, he was so touched he changed his mind and allowed her to go with him. Lisa's actions spoke louder than her words.

God is the same way. Can He see your faith? It's one thing to ask for God's help, but if you want to get God's attention, take it one step further and put actions behind your faith.

## Doors Will Open

> *"Come, follow me,"* Jesus said, *"and I will send you out to fish for people."*
>
> MARK 1:17

A man I know felt called into the ministry. He took a step of faith by renting a small high school auditorium for his first service. He invited his friends and neighbors and spread the word through the town's newspaper, but no one showed up. The only other person was a sound technician. He was so disheartened, but then he thought, "I've taken this step of faith, so I'll give it my all," and he preached his very best. After he finished, a side door opened and a janitor walked down to the front and was joined by the sound technician. Both made a commitment to Christ.

The young minister knew the hand of God was on his life. That was a turning point. Door after door opened after that. Today, he has a church with thousands of people in the congregation.

*When [Jesus] saw [the lepers],*
*he said, "Go, show yourselves to*
*the priests." And as they went,*
*they were cleansed.*

LUKE 17:14

As They
Went

The Scripture tells us that a group of lepers once saw Jesus passing by. They came over and said, "Jesus, please make us well." Jesus could have healed them right there easily enough. But He asked them to do something to express their faith because they were not supposed to be near other people. He said, "Go show yourselves to the priests."

*And as they went,* they were cleansed of their disease. In other words, if they had not had the courage to demonstrate their faith, they would not have seen God's goodness. As they started down the road, I can imagine every few blocks they said, "Can you see it? I think my skin is clearing up." They just kept moving forward, demonstrating their faith, and by the time they reached the priests, they were perfectly normal.

## Steps of Faith

*"Come, let us go over to the garrison of these uncircumcised; it may be that the Lord will work for us. For nothing restrains the Lord from saving by many or by few."*

1 SAMUEL 14:6 NKJV

A lot of times we want change without taking action. "God open the doors, and then I'll step out. Give me the power to break this addiction, then I'll cut back. Give me the big crowds, and then I'll launch my ministry. Let my husband straighten up, and then I'll start treating him better."

You may have a dream that's on hold. You have waited and waited for everything to fall into place, thinking once it does then you'll stretch and make a move. And yes, it's good to have a plan, it's good to stay in God's timing, but you cannot wait around your whole life. At some point you've got to say, "I'm taking a step of faith to put actions behind what I'm believing. I'm going to show God I'm serious about fulfilling my destiny."

## Seek His Kingdom

*"But seek first his kingdom
and his righteousness, and
all these things will be
given to you as well."*

MATTHEW 6:33

Lakewood Church was very crowded in its small auditorium back in 1972. My father had plans drawn for a building that would seat one thousand people. It was estimated to cost about $200,000. He took a special offering for the building fund and received $20,000. But month after month went by with the donations trickling in a few hundred dollars here and there.

One day an old friend of my dad's came by. When he heard about the finances, he looked at my father and said very sternly, "John, pour the foundation and watch what God will do." My father put some actions behind his faith, and they poured the foundation. Before long the money came in for the steel, and then for the exterior. It wasn't any time before the whole building was up and totally paid for.

## Declare God's Protection

*You see that his faith and his actions were working together,*
*and his faith was made complete by what he did.*

JAMES 2:22

When I was a boy, my father traveled overseas for ministry work, often for weeks at a time. Invariably a couple of us kids would either get sick or have an accident while he was away. My mother began to dread him leaving. Finally, he got fed up and said, "God, it's not right that my family is falling apart again." So he decided he would make sure God could see his faith. Instead of just praying over us, he lined all of us kids up outside like a choo-choo train and led us around the perimeter of our property declaring God's protection and had us repeat his words, "No sickness, no disease, and no accidents."

Do you know from that day forward when my father went on those long trips, we never got sick again while he was gone?

## Demonstrate Your Faith

*But do you want to know, O foolish man,*
*that faith without works is dead?*

JAMES 2:20 NKJV

I know good people who have faith and love God, but they're not living an abundant life. They have faith, but it's not doing what it should be doing. It's not helping them overcome obstacles or accomplish dreams. Why is that? Their faith is dead. They're not putting any actions behind it, so it's not activating God's favor.

Your action doesn't have to be something big. When you go to work each day and give it a hundred percent, that's demonstrating your faith. Just the fact that you go to church is an action of faith that God can see. Right now, reading this, you are putting action behind your faith. That tells me your faith is alive and activating God's power. Your faith is allowing God to fight your battles and opening the door for the extraordinary.

## Author and Finisher

*. . . looking unto Jesus, the author and finisher of our faith . . .*

HEBREWS 12:2 NKJV

The moment God put a dream in your heart, the moment the promise took root, God not only started it, but He set a completion date. God is called the author and the finisher of our faith. God wouldn't have given you the dream, the promise wouldn't have come alive, if He didn't already have a plan to bring it to pass.

It doesn't matter how long it's been or how impossible it looks. Your mind may tell you it's too late. You've missed too many opportunities. It's never going to happen. "No," God is saying, "it's not over. I have the final say. I've already set the completion date." If you will stay in faith and not talk yourself out of it, it's just a matter of time before it comes to pass.

*Not one of all the Lord's good promises to Israel failed; every one was fulfilled.*

JOSHUA 21:45

Every
Promise
Fulfilled

Maybe at one time you believed you could do something great, but it's been so long. You tried and it didn't work out. The loan didn't go through. The medical report wasn't good. Now, the "never" lies are playing in your mind. "I'll never get well." "I'll never get married." "I'll never accomplish my dreams."

No, you have to have a new perspective. The Creator of the universe has already set that completion date. Just because it hasn't happened yet doesn't mean it's not going to happen. God has already lined up the right people, the right breaks, the right answers. Everything you need is already in your future. You've got to shake off the doubt and discouragement. Whether it's been a year or fifty years, what God promised you He still has every intention of bringing it to pass.

## Believe, Expect, Know

*It had been revealed to him by the Holy Spirit that he would not die before he had seen the Lord's Messiah.*

LUKE 2:26

# DECEMBER
# 23

Scripture says that it had been revealed to a man named Simeon that he would not die before he had seen the Messiah. You can imagine how far out that promise seemed. As time went by, and Simeon didn't see any sign of the Messiah, I'm sure the negative thoughts came: "You heard wrong. It's been too long. It's never going to happen." Nevertheless, Simeon continued to believe, expect, and know that it would happen, and one day it did. The promise came to a dramatic fulfillment and Simeon declared, "My eyes have seen Your salvation!"

God is saying to you what He said to Simeon: "You need to get ready. I am going to finish what I started. No one and nothing can stop Me from fulfilling My promises. Bad breaks can't stop it. Sickness can't stop it. Death can't even stop it."

## Complete Your Incompletions

*"I prayed for this child, and the LORD has granted me what I asked of him."*

1 SAMUEL 1:27

You need to get ready. God will complete your incompletions. You will not go to your grave without seeing your dreams come to pass—even the secret petitions of your heart. It may seem impossible, but remember, our God is all-powerful. He spoke the worlds into existence, and He has you in the palm of His hand.

God did not create you to be average, to drag through life unfulfilled or unrewarded. He created you to do something amazing. He's put seeds of greatness on the inside. He's whispered things to you in the middle of the night that may seem too big, far out, impossible. But God is saying, "That was My voice. That's My dream for your life. It's bigger; it's more rewarding."

## What Seems Impossible

*Abraham fell facedown; he laughed and said to himself, "Will a son be born to a man a hundred years old? Will Sarah bear a child at the age of ninety?"*

GENESIS 17:17

It may look impossible, but if you'll stay in faith, everything God promised you will come to fulfillment. I met a 106-year-old man who said he was going to be around awhile, because one of his sons has gotten off course. "I can't die yet," he said, "because God promised 'as for me and my house, we will serve the Lord.' I can't go to Heaven until I see God bring every *promise* to pass."

Life will try to push you down, steal your dreams, and talk you into settling for mediocrity. But I want you to have this new attitude and believe that whatever God started in your life, He will finish. Here's the real question: Will you keep believing even though it looks impossible? Will you stay in faith, even though every voice tells you that it's not happening?

> *This is what the LORD says—*
> *your Redeemer, the Holy One*
> *of Israel: "I am the LORD your*
> *God, who teaches you what is*
> *best for you, who directs you in*
> *the way you should go."*
>
> ISAIAH 48:17

# The Right Direction

My pastor friend Jeff Hackelman told me about the time he and some friends were fishing about an hour out in the Gulf of Mexico when a heavy fog suddenly rolled in. The sun started to go down, and in the fog, Jeff lost his sense of direction. All of his logic said, "Go this way," but his friend said, "No, it's that way." Then Jeff remembered his compass, and it showed they were both wrong. The dock was straight north. So against the shouts of his instincts and the panic of his friends, he followed the compass in the total darkness for over an hour and finally spotted land.

There will always be voices trying to convince you that you are headed in the wrong direction or that it's too late to fulfill God's promise. Stay with His promise.

## He Is Trustworthy

*Your kingdom is an everlasting kingdom, and your*
*dominion endures through all generations. The LORD*
*is trustworthy in all he promises and faithful in all he does.*

PSALM 145:13

As we're believing for what God promised us, how many times do we hear messages to the contrary? Sometimes in life, the fog will set in. You won't know if you are headed in the right direction. You know God's put a promise in your heart. But every voice is telling you that you're too old, you missed too many opportunities, and it's not going to happen. In those foggy times, you have to dig in your heels and say, "God, I believe what You promised me despite how I feel, despite what people are telling me, despite how it looks. God, I will believe that what You said is true. I believe You are on the Throne. I know You are a faithful God. What You promised You will bring to pass."

## God Remembers

*God remembered Rachel; he listened to*
*her and enabled her to conceive.*

### GENESIS 30:22

The Scripture says that God put a dream to have a baby in Rachel's heart. But year after year went by, and she couldn't conceive. Rachel remained without a child while her sister, Leah, went on to have one baby after another. Finally, after years of frustration, Rachel grew discouraged and said, in effect, "This is my lot in life. It's never going to happen."

One of the things I love about God is this: Just because we give up on a dream doesn't mean He gives up on it. The Scripture says, "God remembered Rachel." It doesn't say that Rachel remembered God. This is how much God wants you to fulfill your destiny. God is so loving. He's so merciful. Even when we become too discouraged to believe, God does not forget what He promised you.

### Hold to the Hope

*Let us hold unswervingly to the hope we profess, for he who promised is faithful.*

HEBREWS 10:23

When my brother, Paul, was twelve years old, he was in Africa with my father when God planted a dream in his heart that one day he would do medical missions in Africa. Paul went on to become a doctor, and he spent seventeen years as a chief of surgery. After our father died in 1999, Paul felt led to give up his medical practice and help us pastor the church. But God doesn't forget His promises.

In 2009, Paul joined a medical mission to Africa, thinking he'd just be a support. But the other doctors said, "We need you to do these surgeries." He hadn't performed surgery in ten years. Late on his last night there, the thought hit Paul: He was doing what God had put in his heart when he was twelve years old.

*To him who is able to keep you from stumbling and to present you before his glorious presence without fault and with great joy . . .*

JUDE 24

## Final Completion

God knows what He has destined you to do. You may have already said, "Forget it, it will never happen." The good news is, you don't have the final say. God has the final say, and He says, "What I started in your life, I will finish." You may have given up on your dream, but God didn't. What God starts, He will finish. You may not understand how it can happen. It may look like you're too old, you missed too many opportunities, and it's no longer possible. But God has it all figured out. He knows how to connect the dots.

Here's the key: God is not okay with you fulfilling half of your destiny. He's not okay with you fulfilling part of it. God will make sure you complete what He put you here to do.

## Confident of This

*. . . being confident of this, that he who began a good work in you will carry it on to completion until the day of Christ Jesus.*

PHILIPPIANS 1:6

God says that He will complete your incompletions. He remembers the dreams He placed in your heart. He has lined up the right people and the right opportunities. It's not too late. You haven't missed too many opportunities. You haven't made too many mistakes. Get your fire back. Get your passion back. Things have shifted in your favor. God is going to finish what He started.

Now do your part and break out of anything holding you back. Pray God-sized prayers. Don't settle for good enough. *Yes* is in your future. Move forward in faith, and your seeds of greatness will take root. You will go beyond your barriers and become everything God created you to be, and you will have everything He intended for you to have.

# STAY**CONNECTED,**
# BE**BLESSED.**

From thoughtful articles to powerful blogs, podcasts and more, JoelOsteen.com is full of inspirations that will give you encouragement and confidence in your daily life.

AVAILABLE ON JOELOSTEEN.COM

today'sw**O**RD

This daily devotional from Joel and Victoria will help you grow in your relationship with the Lord and equip you to be everything God intends you to be.

**Joel Osteen**
**STREAMING**

Miss a broadcast? Watch Joel Osteen on demand, and see Joel LIVE on Sundays.

**Joel Osteen**
**PODCAST**

The podcast is a great way to listen to Joel where you want, when you want.

## CONNECT WITH US

Join our community of believers on your favorite social network.

## PUT JOEL IN YOUR POCKET

Get the inspiration and encouragement of Joel Osteen on your iPhone, iPad or Android device! Our app puts Joel's messages, devotions and more at your fingertips.

Thanks for helping us make a difference in the lives of millions around the world.

NOTES

NOTES

NOTES